Street Reclaiming

Creating Livable Streets and Vibrant Communities

David Engwicht

NEW SOCIETY PUBLISHERS

Imagine your street
with 50% less traffic.

Imagine cars acting as a guest
in your street.

Imagine your street now transformed
into an "outdoor living room"
with children playing,
neighbors chatting,
and people dancing.

Dream no longer!

Come to the Party

Cataloguing in Publication Data:
A catalog record for this publication is available from the National Library of Canada.

Cover design by Miriam MacPhail.
Book and page design by David Engwicht.
Line drawings by David Engwicht, except for those on pp. 48, 70, 72, 83, 84, 115 and 168 by Michael Gunn.
Cartoons by Les Robinson.

Printed in Canada on acid-free, partially recycled (20 percent post-consumer) paper using soy-based inks by Transcontinental/Best Book Manufacturers.

New Society Publishers acknowledges the financial support of the Government of Canada through the Book Publishing Industry Development Program (BPIDP) for our publishing activities, and the assistance of the Province of British Columbia through the British Columbia Arts Council.

Paperback ISBN: 0-86571-404-5

Inquiries regarding requests to reprint all or part of *Street Reclaiming* should be addressed to New Society Publishers at the address below.

To order directly from the publishers, please add $4.00 shipping to the price of the first copy, and $1.00 for each additional copy (plus GST in Canada). Send check or money order to:

New Society Publishers
P.O. Box 189, Gabriola Island, BC V0R 1X0, Canada

New Society Publishers aims to publish books for fundamental social change through nonviolent action. We focus especially on sustainable living, progressive leadership, and educational and parenting resources. Our full list of books can be browsed on the worldwide web at: http://www.newsociety.com

NEW SOCIETY PUBLISHERS
Gabriola Island BC, Canada

Dedicated

to those who have had the street

as the centre of community life stolen by

excessive traffic:

the artist,

gardener,

conversationalist,

compassionate listener,

actor,

people-watcher,

creative genius,

and playful child —

each of whom

lives in us all.

My brother and me (I'm the eldest).

We must learn how to honor children — and the elderly — in the building of our cities and streets. For only then will we honor the child we once were — and the elder we are yet to become. It is then we will discover the creative potency of combining the past with the future... and play with wisdom.

Meet the Author

Hi. My name is David Engwicht. I live in Brisbane, Australia, on a major road — only because I can't afford to live anywhere else. I was born slap-bang in the middle of the 20th century (I'll leave it to you to work out how old that makes me), but I have a perennial child lurking behind the wicked twinkle in my eye.

In 1987, my life was changed forever when I attended an information meeting about the widening of a road through our suburb. (At the time I was washing windows for a living.) I left the meeting part of a protest group. After giving three years of my life to the fight (we won), I decided to get a real job. But it never happened.

During the campaign I had published two books, both the result of a decision our group made not to push the problem into someone else's back yard, but instead to look for long-term, city-wide solutions. These books thrust me into the international debate on the future of our cities. Next thing I knew I was speaking at conferences and travelling the world helping cities find solutions to their traffic problems.

Then I made a very important discovery: reducing the traffic in our streets is as easy as reducing trash (in Australia we call it rubbish).

I hope you have as much fun taking back your street as I did developing the material for this book over the past four years.

David E

The future is only limited by our imagination — and that is child's play.

CONTENTS

www.lesstraffic.com

ABOUT THIS BOOK

You probably picked up this book because you want less traffic in your street. Like millions of other people world-wide, you are sick and tired of traffic eroding your quality of life with noise and noxious fumes. You are sick and tired of speeding traffic endangering your life, the life of your children, or that of pets.

Or perhaps you are upset by the way traffic just seems to keep growing and taking over the city.

Maybe your house, street, or suburb is currently under threat.

You want your street back. You want solutions. Not some pie-in-the-sky solutions but solutions that ordinary residents like you can implement immediately.

Street reclaiming **is a technological leap beyond traffic calming (speed bumps and chicanes). Not only does it reduce traffic volume and speed in your street, it helps reclaim your street as a place for play, social activity, and community building.**

For thousands of years, streets have been the epicenter of the social, cultural, and economic life of cities. Chapter One reviews this tradition and takes stock of what has been "stolen" by traffic. Rather than doom-and-gloom or a nostalgic look back at the past, this chapter celebrates the potential of our streets. Streets can once again become part of people's "home territory" and play a significant role in their personal growth and sense of belonging. They can become places for community building. They can be reclaimed as the engine-rooms of the creative life of the city, of economic prosperity, and of the democratic process.

In order to reclaim our streets, we first need to dramatically reduce traffic levels. Chapter Two shows that reducing traffic is as simple as reducing trash. By using the *5R's of Traffic Reduction*, we can reduce traffic immediately by about 30% and longer-term by 50% or more — without anyone forgoing a single thing.

However, you don't even need to wait until the traffic levels have dropped on your street before you can start reclaiming it. Chapter Three introduces you to the exciting concept of *psychological reclaiming* — a process of taking back your street immediately with a few simple techniques. Psychological reclaiming builds the base for *physical reclaiming,* a process of taking back the physical

Why is it that people don't dance in the street today?
Christopher Alexander *A Pattern Language*

Calling out around the world: "Are you ready for the brand new beat?"
This is an invitation across the nation, a chance for folks to meet,
There'll be laughing, singing, and music swinging,
Dancing in the streets.
Martha and the Vandellas

If some day Americans should want to opt for a more dignified city life, the street will be first on the list to come in for rehabilitation.

Bernard Rudofsky, *Streets for People*

space freed up through reduced car use. Chapter Three presents a smorgasbord of design ideas for both the psychological and physical reclaiming of your street.

Chapter Four gives an overview of a process that you and a couple of neighbors can initiate to reclaim your street. In just five to seven weeks, you can have your street back.

Chapter Five shows how the concepts and practical steps outlined in this book help to tackle the root causes of traffic problems. It does so by exposing eight myths that underpin current approaches to urban and transport planning. This chapter shows how street reclaiming is built on a whole new approach.

Chapter Six asks the question, "Are our streets worth saving?" It concludes that we must not just reclaim a lost tradition — we must rebuild our streets so that they help us face the challenges of the future.

This book is not anti-car. It is a celebration of what your street and city could be like with less traffic and slower speeds. And it shows you how this can be achieved in a practical, down-to-earth way.

But this is more than just a book about reclaiming the streets we live on. It is about reclaiming a civil society, a compassionate society which sustains the well-being of all its citizens. It is about reclaiming a sense of community in an age of globalization. It is about reclaiming our cities as a place where great civilizations are born and nurtured. It is about reclaiming our creative powers and not allowing the past or present to dictate the future. It is about starting every journey with a sense of wonder and adventure.

THANKS...

This book is a result of four years development of the *Traffic Reduction Kit*. Special thanks go to

- Australia Council, Australia's art funding body, for a grant which helped develop the earliest versions of the *Traffic Reduction Kit*;
- Brisbane City Council, particularly Cr Maureen Hayes, for support in running the first kit trial;
- Residents of Henry Street, Wooloowin (Brisbane), not just for participating in the first Kit trial,

but for making suggestions which improved the Kit substantially. Much of their wisdom is reflected in this book;

- Northern Rivers Social Development Council for funding a trial of the Kit in Lismore, Australia;
- Council and government staff worldwide who looked at early versions of the Kit and made practical suggestions for its improvement;
- My friends and supporters in many parts of the world, some of whom gave me lodging and support. Each

of you owns a little part of this book. A special thanks to Craig and Carla Anderson, Chris DeMarco, and Dan Burden.

- Ingrid Burkett, my best mate, who encouraged me to continue when I wanted to throw in the towel, shared a journey to unlock the secrets of streets in Europe, and offered invaluable feedback on the text in this book;
- Luke, Jodi, and Nathan, my three children, who have endured my obsessions.

chapter one

ROBBED BLIND

Taking Stock of What Has Been Stolen

The urban environment should again become a place favorable to human encounter; for looking around, listening and talking to people, walking about and sitting down. Streets and squares should once again be treated as outside rooms within the city, as places where the opportunity of contact between people is the primary consideration.

Jan Tanghe, et al., *Living Cities*

Did you notice something missing?

Why do you want less traffic on your street or in your neighborhood?

Like many others, you probably find traffic obnoxious. It is like an unwelcome guest that has barged into your private space. It is noisy, smelly, and intimidating.

But look closely, and you will find that this unwelcome guest has done more than make you feel uncomfortable in your own space. It has subverted the traditional roles of the street — roles that have been considered invaluable to a functioning society for thousands of years.

This chapter examines some of the traditional roles of the street and discusses the importance of these traditions for a healthy society and for healthy individuals. It shows how traffic has eroded these traditional roles.

However, this chapter is not a nostalgic pining for a glorified past. I acknowledge that the past had imperfections just like the present. Rather, I look back in order to look forward. There was an inherent wisdom and logic in the traditional roles of the street. In trying to build a better future, we would be extremely foolish to cut ourselves off from this insight.

Neither does this chapter engage in a witch-hunt against the car. At its heart is a celebration — a celebration of the role that streets could once again play in our social, cultural and economic life. What I hope to do here is to inspire you to begin the process of reclaiming your street.

The loss and reclaiming of 'home territory'

For centuries, people have felt that the street in front of their house was an important part of their home territory. "Home" was not just the dwelling in which they ate, slept, and procreated. "Home" embraced the street on which people lived, the marketplace, the street leading to the market place, the landmarks, the public buildings, and dozens of special places. But the street outside one's house was a very special part of this extended sense of home. It was a place where the chatter and laughter of neighborhood children could be heard; a place where the elderly sat, dispensing their wisdom and admonishing the children if they got out of hand; a place to sit and watch the drama of life being played out in the faces of both acquaintances and those journeying through; a place for conversation, debate, and even protest; a place for celebrating the coming and going of seasons; a place to mark the important stages of life from birth to death.

As I can't leap from cloud to cloud, I want to wander from road to road. That little path there by the clipped hedge goes up to the high road. I want to go up that path and to walk along the high road, and so on and on and on, and know all kinds of people. Did you ever think that the roads are the only things that are endless; that one can walk on and on, and never be stopped by a gate or a wall? They are the serpent of eternity. I wonder they have never been worshipped. What are the stars beside them? They never meet one another. The roads are the only things that are infinite. They are endless.

Yeats

In many European cultures, the occupants of houses ritualistically swept the street in front of their homes. This piece of street, while public, held a special place in their affections. In the map of their minds, it was part of their home territory — their outdoor living room.

The importance of the home territory tradition

Home territory provided a strong sense of place. And a sense of place can be very important in developing our identity as people. A sense of place is a feeling of affinity with the physical environment. The elements that make up our physical environment become the repository of our memories and affections and therefore cease to be merely physical elements, but grow into an essential part of our mental landscape. A bench ceases to be just a bench if it is where we stole our first kiss or where we had an intriguing conversation with an eccentric stranger. A tree ceases to be a just a tree if we played in it as a child or stopped off on our way home from school to eat its fruit. A street ceases to be just a street if it is where we met an elderly person who enriched our life with wisdom and tales of the past. The bench, the tree, or the street become part of us, and we become part of them. Even if the bench, tree, or street cease to exist in the physical realm, they live on as special place in our memories. Every time we see them or use them or conjure them up in our imagination, we "come home." They become a safe haven where our identity is reconfirmed.

A sense of place also helps build a sense of identity through social interactions. Home territory, and its attached sense of place, is shared by a community of people. In fact, it is the social interactions within a space (more than the elements of that space) which give it its sense of place and home.

Within a properly functioning community, each individual gives specific "gifts" to the other members of the community. These may be gifts of leadership, a listening ear, wisdom, a smile, or watching the kids playing on the sidewalk. It is in the giving of gifts to others, and the acceptance of those gifts by others, that our identity is affirmed. In traditional urban cultures, the street immediately outside one's home, together with the marketplace, were the chief places for this mutual exchange of gifts.

Home territory therefore helps develop our identity by giving us a strong attachment to our physical environment and by providing a setting for community building through the exchange of gifts. Both are essential to our emotional, spiritual, and psychological well-being.

How traffic erodes the home-territory tradition

In 1970, Donald Appleyard conducted some ground-breaking research in San Francisco. He chose three residential streets which, on the surface, were identical, except for their levels of traffic. One street carried 2,000 vehicles per day and was called Light Street in his study. Another carried 8,000 and was called Medium Street. The other carried 16,000 and was called Heavy Street. He asked people to indicate where their friends and acquaintances lived in their streets. Those on Light Street reported having three times more friends and twice as many acquaintances on their streets as those on Heavy Street (Figure 1.1).

A clue as to why the people on Heavy Street had three times less friends and acquaintances than the people on Light Street emerged when Appleyard asked residents to draw on the map of their street what they considered to be their "home territory" (Figure 1.2). The results were dramatic. Those with light traffic on their street marked out a territory which covered the entire road and both sidewalks. Those on Heavy Street never marked the road as part of their home territory. Few marked anything past their own front yard. As speed and volume of traffic increased, the area people considered to be their home territory shrank.

Appleyard discovered that traffic does not just take over physical space. It has a "zone of influence" which intimidates and takes over a space psychologically. Through observations Appleyard documented how, as the speed and

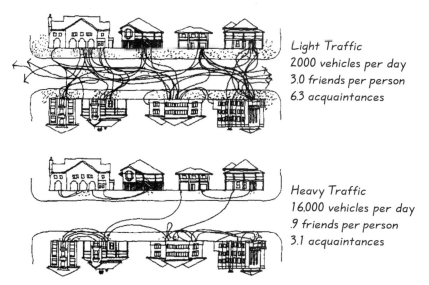

Light Traffic
2000 vehicles per day
3.0 friends per person
6.3 acquaintances

Heavy Traffic
16,000 vehicles per day
.9 friends per person
3.1 acquaintances

Fig. 1.1. Lines show where people said they had friends or acquaintances. (Adapted from D. Appleyard, Livable Streets.)

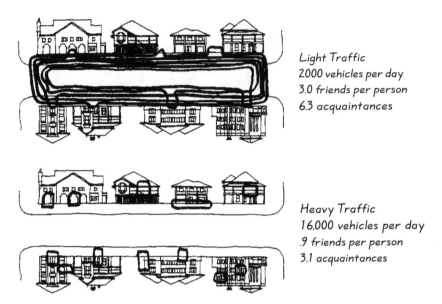

Light Traffic
2000 vehicles per day
3.0 friends per person
6.3 acquaintances

Heavy Traffic
16,000 vehicles per day
.9 friends per person
3.1 acquaintances

Fig. 1.2. Lines show areas people considered to be their 'home territory'. (Adapted from D. Appleyard, Livable Streets.)

There was nothing like it before in history: a machine that promised liberation from the daily bondage of place. And in a free country like the United States, with the unrestricted right to travel, a vast geographical territory to spread out into, and a national tradition of picking up and moving whenever life at home became intolerable, the automobile came as a blessing. In the early years of motoring, hardly anyone understood the automobile's potential for devastation — not just of the landscape, or the air, but of culture in general.

James Howard Kunstler, *The Geography of Nowhere*

volume of traffic increased, the zone of influence grew and the home territory shrank. On Light Street the children still played in the carriageway and people would stop there to talk. But as traffic increased, these activities moved to the sidewalk. As the traffic increased further, the function of the sidewalk changed from being a space for play and socializing to being a space used "solely as a corridor between the sanctuary of individual homes and the outside world." This abandonment of the sidewalk as a space for socializing creates a vicious circle. Children and adults abandon this space because it is dirty, dangerous, and noisy. The removal of these activities makes the space even more barren and increases the feelings that it is some kind of alien and dangerous territory. So it is abandoned even further.

However, Appleyard found that the shrinking of home territory did not stop at the sidewalk. On Heavy Street, there was a dramatic decrease in the number of people gardening or simply sitting on their front steps. Nor did the shrinking stop at the front steps. Many people on Heavy Street had abandoned the front rooms of their dwellings, using them more as a buffer between the street and the back rooms of the house. Thus, some people on Heavy Street had even lost parts of their internal living space as part of their home territory.

One reason people on Heavy Street had fewer social contacts is precisely because they had less territory in which to transact social exchanges.

The last step in this saga of shrinking home territory was that some people abandoned their homes altogether, thereby disrupting existing social networks. This, combined with the shrinking home territory, explained why people on Heavy Street had fewer social contacts in their street. According to Appleyard, people on Heavy Street tended to treat their street as a transient hotel rather than a residence. Appleyard concluded his study with this observation: "The contrast between the two streets [Heavy and Light] was striking. On the one hand alienation, on the other friendliness and involvement."

Traffic erodes home territory, and with it a sense of home and personal identity.

Looking to the future

We live in an age of increasing mobilization and globalization. Our streets have been widened to accommodate the extra mobility. They become like every other clogged traffic artery anywhere else in the world. Residents move out and the international burger franchise stores move in. Our neighborhood begins to lose its distinctive feel and becomes part of a global culture.

In a world of increasing globalization, the need for a strong home territory — with its own distinctive personality — becomes even more pressing. This does not mean that we should reject some of the benefits that come with increased mobility and globalization but rather that the detrimental effects of these trends must be balanced through creating a stronger home territory. In other words, it is possible to belong to a global community without being swallowed up and losing our unique, local identity. It is possible to belong to two communities: the global community and a local community.

However, building local community requires local spaces. Traditionally, this role was fulfilled by the streets and squares. This book argues that this is still the logical choice.

America is not Europe. We don't have thousand-year-old cathedral plazas and market squares. In general, our public realm is the street, and we've turned it into a national automobile slum.

James Howard Kunstler, "*Fighting Words form the US of A*"

Celebrating the return of your home territory

Street Reclaiming means refusing to be intimidated by traffic and asserting your right to your street as an integral part of your home territory — a place for play, social interaction, and community building.

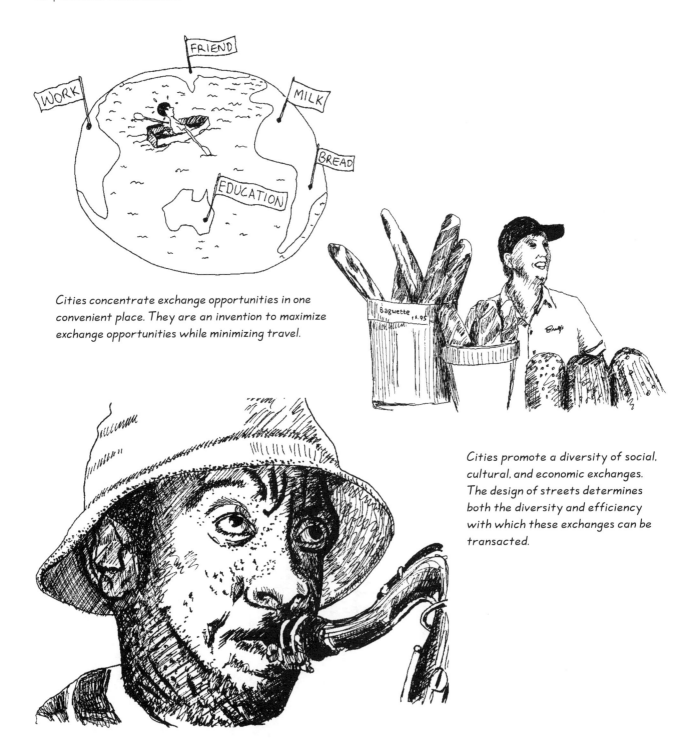

Cities concentrate exchange opportunities in one convenient place. They are an invention to maximize exchange opportunities while minimizing travel.

Cities promote a diversity of social, cultural, and economic exchanges. The design of streets determines both the diversity and efficiency with which these exchanges can be transacted.

The Loss and Reclaiming of Exchange Space

In *Reclaiming Our Cities and Towns (Towards an Eco-City)*, I went back to the most fundamental questions of all: why do we build cities, and what is the role of the transport system in a city. I defined a city as an invention to maximize exchange opportunities and to minimize travel. These exchanges may be exchanges of goods, friendship, knowledge, culture, work, education or emotional and spiritual support. We choose to live in cities because exchanges are the real stuff of life. As humans, we crave reciprocal relationships, new ideas, and surroundings that stimulate all our senses. Cities are a deliberate concentration of these exchange opportunities in order to increase both the diversity and accessibility of exchange opportunities. Instead of these exchange opportunities being scattered all over the globe, they are concentrated in one convenient place.

However, we still need to move to gain access to these exchange opportunities — all be it, not as far as if they were scattered all over the globe. This means that cities cannot just be a concentration of exchange opportunities; they must devote some of their space to movement. Cities are therefore composed of two types of space: exchange space and movement space. Now, the more space a city devotes to movement, the more the exchange space becomes diluted and scattered (Figure 1.3). The more diluted and scattered the exchange opportunities, the more the city begins to lose the very thing that makes it a city: a concentration of exchange opportunities. What makes a city efficient, and an exciting place to be, is this diversity and density of potential exchanges.

One of the ways cities historically increased their efficiency and the density and diversity of exchange opportunities was to use streets as a dual space for both movement and exchange. While making journeys on foot or bicycle, people would engage in a wide range of spontaneous social, cultural and economic exchanges. Public transport continued this dual use of space. There were plenty of opportunities for spontaneous exchanges on the walk to the public transport stop, and while riding with others.

This notion of streets existing not just for movement but also for exchange was built into the very structure of older city streets. Wander around the core of any European city and you will find that the streets are a series of "outdoor rooms" connected by "corridors" (see feature box next page). Even the corridors can often be viewed as small rooms. You wander down a narrow passageway and suddenly it opens out into a larger space. This may be a square, or the room may simply be the result of the way the buildings have grown up organically over centuries. It is in these outdoor rooms that you find people sitting, that you see outdoor cafes, market stalls,

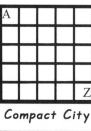

Compact City

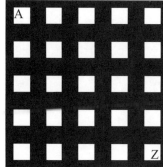

Big-Roads-n-Carparks City

Fig. 1.3 Both these cities have the same amount of exchange space (white area). However, the exchange spaces are more scattered in the second city because it devotes more of its space to movement (black road and carparking space). The people who live at A are therefore forced to travel further to access the exchange at Z.

buskers, etc. From inside this room you will see a number of "doorways" leading off into passageways or streets that connect to the next room. This structure encourages people to pause in each room to consider if they should participate in one or more of the exchange opportunities offered there and then puts people in the position of having to make a decision: which way now?

Venice—outdoor rooms

The city grew on small adjacent islands built up from the marsh lagoon. Originally, every tiny island was a self contained community, with its own church, with houses around the edge, and a large open space or "campo" in the centre for social and community activities, for the market, and for secular and religious festivities.

Some centuries after these island communities were formed, bridges were built and narrow passages created to link the communities together. This pattern of community living spaces, or "campi," and a city wide pedestrian network survived intact today, little changed since the fifteenth century ....

Entering a campo one has the distinct feeling that one has arrived at a place. The campo is entirely surrounded by buildings. There is no view out of the campo and no immediately visible exit. The surrounding buildings seem like walls enclosing an outdoor room: they help focus attention inwards on the activity within the campo .... This architectural arrangement is highly theatrical: the campo is like an enlarged Shakespearian theatre, in which all the people at the balconies and windows as well as those on the campo are at the same moment both audience and actors ....

One of the most unique features of the Venetian campo is that it is both a public space and a semi-private space. It is public because streets and alleys lead into it, there is no gate, nor any other kind of barrier, so Ventians from other districts and tourists can walk into the campo. On the other hand, as any visitor immediately senses, the campo is like an outdoor room, a territory which belongs to the community in general and in particular to each of the inhabitants ....

Every campo has its own unique character, its own special blend of social life which derives from its local population and from its location within Venice.

From Suzanne Crowhurst-Lennard and Henry L Lennard "Public Life in Urban Spaces: The Lessons of the Venetian Campo" in *Proceedings: Sixth Annual Pedestrian Conference*, Boulder 1985.

The importance of the exchange-space tradition

The city was an important step in society's evolution. It increased the diversity of exchange opportunities, which, as we shall see later, increased the creative potential of civilization. To modern urban planners, the organic street patterns of older European cities seem chaotic and inefficient. However, they only appear this way if your goal is to improve the efficiency of movement within the city. If your goal is to increase the diversity of exchange opportunities and the efficiency with which these exchanges can be transacted, then the organic street patterns have their inherent logic.

Corridors in a house, which can only be used for movement, are often referred to as wasted space. They are considered a waste because what we value about our house is not the movement between rooms but the activities facilitated by the rooms: meals with our family or friends, a sunny corner to read a book, soaking in a hot bath, a night of passion before sinking into sleep. As much as possible, good house design minimizes corridors and maximizes room space. To achieve this goal, rooms take on the dual function of movement space and living space. The inherent logic of the organic street layout of older cities was that it adopted this design principle from internal dwellings. Streets performed the dual function of movement space and living space, minimizing the space used purely for movement. This allowed the city to fulfill its mission of delivering diversity of exchange opportunities much more efficiently. The higher density of exchange opportunities meant that journeys were both shorter and more interesting. In addition, the

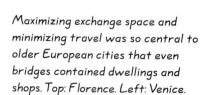

Maximizing exchange space and minimizing travel was so central to older European cities that even bridges contained dwellings and shops. Top: Florence. Left: Venice.

A typical "outdoor room" in Bologna, Italy. Note how the changes in pavement design break the space up into smaller rooms but also delinate movement paths through the space.

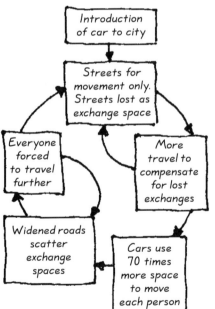

Fig. 1.4 The vicious circle that erodes exchange opportunities and scatters the city

organic layout meant that there were many combinations of routes in getting from point A to B — again making each journey more interesting and increasing the variety of exchanges one could potentially engage in.

How traffic erodes the exchange-space tradition

The introduction of the car produced a double blow to the overall exchange efficiency of the city. Firstly, it converted the dual function of streets into a single function: that of movement. This is like taking the rooms in a house, removing the furniture, and declaring that they are now a corridor for movement. Converting the dual function of streets to a single function not only destroyed the spontaneous social, cultural, and economic exchanges that once took place in the street, it eroded the home territory on which these exchanges could be transacted. Secondly, movement by car demanded at least 70 times more road space to move each person than when people walked. This extra space could only be obtained by handing over more of the city to movement space which in reality meant destroying exchange spaces and converting these into movement space. This put the whole city into a vicious circle (Figure 1.4). Destinations were scattered and everyone forced to travel more to try and compensate for lost exchanges. This extra traffic further eroded and diluted exchange opportunities.

Looking to the future

Cities are threatening a major ecological disaster. They are consuming valuable farm-land and natural environments as they spread out. The forced extra traffic is generating emissions that are the chief contributor to global warming. The tradition of seeing cities as an invention to maximize exchange opportunities while minimizing costs gives us a basis for building more ecologically sustainable cities. The first step is to restore the dual functions of the streets as places for both exchange and movement. If we do this, we will reap more than just more sustainable cities. Our neighborhoods and cities will become more lively, interesting, and stimulating places to live. We will spend less time traveling and more time enjoying the reasons for which we travel.

Dorris Harris, aged 84, had lived in this house since she was twenty. It was bulldozed to widen a road for cars. This is an act of destroying destinations — in the act of trying to get to them.

When the last box had been packed and sealed and carried out, she slowly walked around her empty house and through the garden, both now destined for the bulldozers... She was pale and visibly trembling as she was gently helped into a waiting car. Her budgie and three cats were beside her...

Nathalie Hayman, *Resumed in Protest*

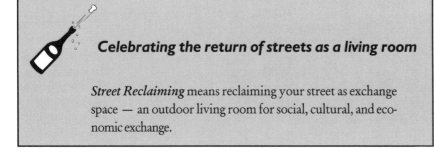

Celebrating the return of streets as a living room

Street Reclaiming means reclaiming your street as exchange space — an outdoor living room for social, cultural, and eco-nomic exchange.

The Loss and Reclaiming of Spontaneity

There are two kinds of exchanges transacted in the city: planned and spontaneous exchanges. Planned exchanges are the ones we make a deliberate journey for: a trip to the shop to get milk, a trip to the bank to arrange a loan, a trip to school to get an education. Spontaneous exchanges usually get transacted while making a trip to a planned exchange: we bump into an old friend who tells us news about mutual friends, we see a notice in a shop window calling a protest meeting over council plans to sell the local park, we see a lounge chair in a shop window that takes our fancy so we have it put aside for us, we pass people in the street and they evoke storytelling in our head and we in theirs. The social, cultural, and economic exchanges that take place in the street and public squares (the dual exchange/movement space) are largely spontaneous.

The importance of the tradition of spontaneity

If cities are an invention to increase the diversity of exchange opportunities and the efficiency with which these are made use of, then the spontaneous exchange is foundational. In the course of making a journey to transact a single planned exchange, someone may be involved in dozens of spontaneous exchanges along the way. As we have seen, organic streets were structured in a way that deliberately encourages a rich diversity of these spontaneous exchange opportunities. There is a tendency in the mentality of industrial society to write these dozens of spontaneous exchanges off as trivial. In later sections of this chapter we will explore how these spontaneous exchanges are fundamental to the creative life of the city; the personal development of the citizens, including their emotional and spiritual well-being; the equity with which people have access to the exchanges offered by the city; the democratic process; and economic prosperity.

For now let us explore just one benefit of these spontaneous exchanges, one articulated by Jane Jacobs in her classic *The Death and Life of Great American Cities*. She describes how in her neighborhood in New York people would leave their house keys with a local storekeeper to be handed over to someone coming to do repairs or to guests that may be arriving while the home-owner was out. She then asks the question: where does this level of trust originate? Here is her own answer:

> The trust of a city is formed over time from many, many sidewalk contacts ...
> Most of it is ostensibly utterly trivial but the sum is not trivial at all. The sum
> of such casual, public contact at a local level ... is a feeling for the public
> identity of people, a web of public respect and trust, and a resource in time of

She rode into my life on a scooter
out of the blue
and unannounced.
Twelve months later she was gone
leaving invaluable gifts
I will treasure forever.

personal or neighborhood need. The absence of this trust is a disaster to a city street ... Lowly, unpurposeful and random as they may appear, sidewalk contacts are the small change from which a city's wealth of public life may grow.

Spontaneous exchanges which take place in the street are therefore crucial in building an informal network of support within a neighborhood. In fact, the whole quality of neighborhood life is largely built from these spontaneous exchanges.

How traffic erodes the tradition of spontaneity

We have seen from Appleyard's research that traffic psychologically takes over the space traditionally used for spontaneous encounters. Ironically, the people on Heavy Street have their home territory — the chief place for spontaneous encounters — eroded by people in cars who are in the process of making a journey to transact a planned exchange. The only way that people on Heavy Street can replace these lost spontaneous exchanges is via a planned exchange — which in many cases involves them driving down someone else's street and destroying their opportunities for spontaneous encounters. This produces a vicious circle (Figure 1.5) which gradually destroys the spontaneous exchange realm of the city and moves the city towards higher and higher reliance on planned exchanges.

There is another subtle way in which traffic destroys the spontaneous encounter realm of the city. Private cars allow people to enter and pass through public space encased in a "privacy capsule." This robs not only the occupants in the car but also other people of the opportunity for spontaneous exchanges alone the way, be that on the street or on public transport. As we shall discover when talking about the role of "people-watching", the ability to observe others (even if no words are exchanged) is a powerful stimulus to our personal growth and creative wealth. Allowing people to enter the public domain in a privacy capsule dilutes the essential nature of the city as a place of diverse exchange opportunities.

Many people misinterpret what reclaiming the spontaneous domain of the city really means. Some think I am trying to force them into not driving to the beach on the weekend (a planned exchange) and instead to stay home and interact spontaneously with their neighbors. "What if I don't like my neighbors?" they ask. But the real issue is *diversity of choice*. If streets were reclaimed and the spontaneous domain reinstated, people would have a *choice* between a planned day at the beach or staying home and having a game of street hockey with the neighbors, or a quiet conversation. At the moment, the latter option may not exist, which restricts our choices to planned exchanges. And for many citizens without access to a car, even the planned exchange options are severely limited.

Others see real advantages in being able to enter public space encased in a privacy machine. They see it as a way of avoiding unwanted "spontaneous exchanges." This response demonstrates just how much we have actually lost contact with what streets were once like and how they could be again. Where streets have been abandoned to traffic, they do become dangerous places where the "spontaneous encounter" is more likely to be threatening than exciting.

But where streets are operating as outdoor rooms full of activity, the strong presence of others actually provides a greater degree of freedom and flexibility in personal relationships than one has in a city where streets have been abandoned to cars. In a city with a vibrant street life, if you wish to hold a conversation with someone new, you can do so in the street, under the watchful gaze of others. In cities with no street life, if you wish to hold a conversation with a stranger, you must do so in more "private" space — for example, your room. If you invite a stranger into your house to get to know them, ending the conversation is much harder than if you are conducting the same conversation in the street, under the watchful eye of others. In vibrant public domains, the spontaneous encounter is not one we are forced to endure. We can more easily terminate or avoid an encounter. Ironically, enlarging the spontaneous encounter realm of the city allows us also to reclaim our private spaces. Because we have two living rooms (one inside and one outside), the first encounters with others, and the building of these relationships, can take place in the safety of our outdoor living room. We get to choose if and when we want to invite people into our inside living room. A vibrant spontaneous public realm therefore allows greater flexibility in our private relationships. Some people, maybe even a majority of people, can be kept as nodding acquaintances without them ever invading the private space of our house.

The car, and the death of the spontaneous encounter realm, forces us into what Sennet called "polarized intimacy." Instead of there being a continuum of intimacy in our relationships extending from the bedroom to nodding acquaintances in the street, the middle ground is removed and we are forced into an intimacy gamble — all or nothing. As Jane Jacobs observed, more often than not, when faced with the choice of

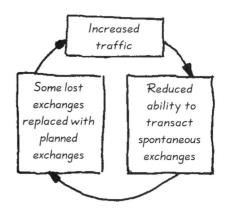

Fig. 1.5 How traffic erodes the spontaneous exchanges of the city and moves to an increasing reliance on planned exchanges. Over time, this circle results in a net loss of exchanges that can be transacted.

It has all too often slipped our minds that a sense of fun and a large measure of irrationality can be as meaningful as the development of knowledge. The structure of attractive cities is sometimes very irrational by modern standards of efficient and rational planning, but the true values in life often seem to stem from the unforeseen and the unplanned. The best cities are like the best parties; nobody planned them in advance and that is why they are so successful.

Jan Tanghe, et al, *Living Cities*

A city doesn't get its character from brassy new hotels with space-capsule elevators gliding up the walls.

Nor does character come from Astrodomes or from phallic monuments to architectural egos.

Character comes from people, from the past, from tradition, from the interplay of human forces and emotions in the process of daily life.

It springs from the bazaars and marketplaces, the why and how cities began, where people could meet, buy, exchange, communicate, work, carouse, steal, fight, love, relax, be entertained and learn.

Ivan Menzies — *Boston Globe,* March 24, 1976, in Roberta Brandes Gratz , in *The Living City*

sharing much or nothing, people chose nothing: "If mere contact with your neighbors threatens to entangle you in their private lives, or entangle them in yours ... the logical solution is absolutely to avoid friendliness or casual offers of help" (p.65). A tragic result of this polarized intimacy and the loss of casual contact is that we cease to build trust between the people in a neighborhood. As a result, informal support mechanisms fail. And the public jobs, like keeping an eye on the children playing on the sidewalk, don't get done. It is these webs of mutual support and the taking of responsibility for the quality of neighborhood life which are the hallmarks of a civilized society. They also give to the individuals a strong sense of identity.

Looking to the future

In visioning exercises I have done with people in both Australia and North America, I have asked people to create stories about the kinds of cities they would like to be living in 20 years from now. Consistently there have been two central elements to the stories people create: a more convenient city with a wide range of facilities "just around the corner" and an increase in human contact.

These two elements are combined in one story created by a group of people who had adopted the role of a single mum with two children. They presented their story as a reading from this young woman's diary. She wrote: "This morning I called 'Ronny's Hot Bagels' to have some hot bagels delivered. It was not so much the bagels that I was looking forward to, but Ronny's smile."

In a society that has become increasingly atomised, with traditional extended family links weakened, the need for casual contact is perhaps now greater than ever. In order for us to build a humane, compassionate city, the return of the spontaneous realm to our streets is the first step.

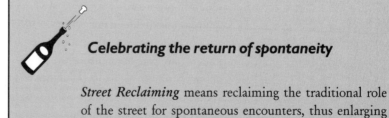

Celebrating the return of spontaneity

Street Reclaiming means reclaiming the traditional role of the street for spontaneous encounters, thus enlarging our choice of exchanges and building a strong web of relationships.

The Loss and Return of a Stimulus to Creative Wealth

The creation of anything new requires a new combination of two or more elements. This is why we as a society have come to value diversity. Diversity increases the number of potential combinations or marriages exponentially. Diversity therefore increases the chances that a new combination may produce a new life form that can meet the challenges of a changing environment.

However, no new life forms can emerge in a totally ordered world, regardless of the extent of diversity. A certain level of chaos (randomness or spontaneity if the word *chaos* frightens you) is essential in order for the diverse elements to bump into each other, to form new relationships and, from these new relationships, to evolve new life-forms. In evolution, chaos is the matchmaker of diversity. It provides the introductions and meeting ground for new relationships to form. In nature, chaos also disrupts existing relationships, which opens up the possibility for the elements to form new relationships which are potentially more beneficial than the current ones.

In evolution, the development of the city was a quantum leap forward for creativity. It increased diversity and provided the spontaneity or chaos necessary for this diversity to mix and form new relationships. The city was a cooperative enterprise in which people were free to do what they did best. The tillers of soil grew food, the herdsmen tended their flocks, philosophers and priests pondered the meaning of life, craftpersons and artisans shared their knowledge and developed new products that improved the quality of life, and artists created plays and works of art that acted as mirrors to society. The street was the mediator of this burgeoning creative life — the place where food, philosophy, practical products, art, wisdom, and fantasy mingled. There were no clear divides between these realms because each acted as a stimulus to the other.

The importance of the tradition of creative wealth

Let's examine just two important outcomes of a diverse, spontaneous street life as a stimulus to creative wealth. Firstly, the economic well-being of the entire city depends on its creative wealth. New products, better products, and smarter ways of doing business all have their genesis in the creative life of the city. Times change. Economies change. Cities that do not have a vibrant creative life lack adaptability and fossilize.

Secondly, our personal growth is dependent on this creative milieu. Our exposure to diversity in the city is not always experienced as a pleasant stimulus. The encounter with another person's world often collides head on with our prejudices, beliefs, and

What we are drawn to in cities is the potential of human contact, the multiplicity of opportunities, the socio-cultural diversity. These elements stimulate human creativity, provide the pluralistic basis for a community, and make the public environment our open house.

Ray Bradbury, in Roberto Brambilla, *More Streets for People*

Eccentrics add colour and life to the street. They can provoke us into viewing the world through new eyes.

Exposure to diversity, and the integration of that diversity into our mental landscape, is the key to personal growth.

personal mythologies. This can be interpreted as either a threat or a challenge to personal growth. Every time our carefully crafted belief system is challenged, we are opened to the possibility of developing a new synthesis — a whole new way of viewing the world. This is the creative process of nature: it brings previously unrelated worlds into contact and, at the meeting point of those two worlds, creates new life. These spontaneous encounters are therefore essential to our ongoing growth and to the development of a much more robust and sustainable mental life.

How traffic erodes the tradition of creative wealth

We are currently on a vicious treadmill. We have taken the creative crucible of the city — its streets — and handed them over to a form of movement which destroys both the essential elements of creativity: diversity and spontaneity (or good chaos). We are forced to rely increasingly on planned exchanges for our interactions. With planned exchanges we can insulate ourselves from encounters that may challenge our carefully crafted belief system. However, by so doing, we lose the ability to integrate new experiences of life. And so we erect stronger defences against the unknown. Our belief systems lose their elasticity and harden. The spontaneous realm of the city becomes a threat rather than a promoter of new life. So we wind the windows of the car up, put on the air-conditioning, pipe in some music, and drive into our gated community.

But the certainty that we have embraced is the certainty of extinction. New life is only ever generated where previously unrelated worlds are allowed to mix and form new relationships. In this territory nothing is predictable. New life waits in this risky and uncertain marginal territory where our world collides head on with other people's worlds. To embrace a world that is totally ordered and predictable is to withdraw into our shell and wait for death.

Looking to the future

We live in a world of rapid change. In times of rapid change we tend to grasp for anchors — still points in the storm of change. Ironically, the grasp for certainty reduces our ability to meet the challenges presented by this fast-changing world.

The solution, I believe, would be an environment that uses spontaneity as a means of providing a sense of attachment while still acting as a stimulus to creativity. As noted in the previous section, the spontaneous exchange can help build a web of trust and attachment at the local level. This web of trust gives to the individual a sense of belonging. At the same time, the spontaneous encounters that build this web carry within them the possibility of provoking personal growth and creativity. If the primary realm for the transaction of spontaneous exchanges is

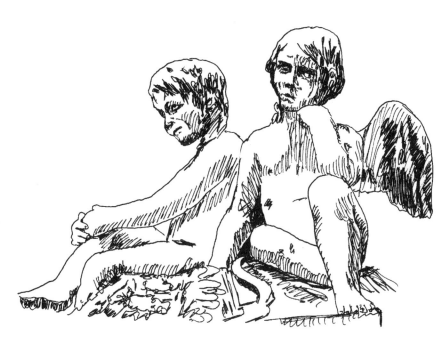

The street itself has been the great world theatre. Drama and comedy, both spontaneous and contrived, were supplied by daily life... Not by accident did Scamozzi [Itally 1579] choose a streetscape as permanent backdrop of what is considered the first modern playhouse... The street has always been the favorite setting of the full-blooded playwright; wisdom utters her voice in the street.

Bernard Rudofsky, *Streets for People*

the local neighborhood, then this provides a supportive environment in which the spontaneous encounter becomes less threatening.

There is no doubt we live in challenging times. Feeding the creative wealth of the city is therefore paramount. This means reclaiming our streets as places rich in diverse exchange opportunities, as places of spontaneity and creativity.

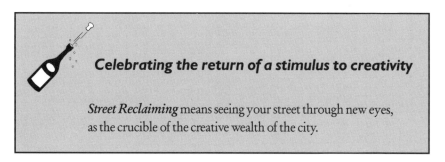

Celebrating the return of a stimulus to creativity

Street Reclaiming means seeing your street through new eyes, as the crucible of the creative wealth of the city.

The Loss and Return of Children's Play Space

For millennia the street was the premier playground for children. Supervision was a community responsibility. A mother would sit on her doorstep shelling peas keeping an eye on proceedings. An elderly man sitting on a chair brought out onto the sidewalk would call out and pull those into line who were getting boisterous or causing others a nuisance. The play would involve children of all ages.

The importance of the tradition of children's street play

Many people in the USA, Canada, UK, and Australia consider that the street is not a place where children should play. Modern children have a backyards, playgrounds, organized sport, and a rumpus room in the house. Children who traditionally played in the street were forced to do so because they did not have the same opportunities as the modern child. In fact, "street kids" and "in the gutter" have become euphemisms for disadvantage. But I believe there is a pressing necessity to reclaim the street for children's play. There are a number of benefits of street play which can never be compensated for by parks, backyards, organized sport, or rumpus rooms. These benefits include:

Mental Stimuli: In *The Experience of Place,* Tony Hiss discusses the research of Dr. Marian Diamond and her colleagues at the University of California in Berkeley. Young rats that were placed in an enriched environment — one with plenty of toys and playmates — started growing bigger brains in just a few days, while the cortex of young rats confined to an impoverished environment shrank in size. But according to Dr. Diamond, the rats in the enriched environment did not just have bigger brains. They were more intelligent, being better able to run mazes. "The main factor is stimulation," she says. "Nerve cells are designed to receive stimulation" (p.38). Similarly, the traditional street was an "enriched environment" full of characters, action, and movement. These stimuli were important in the mental development of children.

Back in 1928, the Regional Plan Association of New York reported on the difficulty of getting children to use parks rather than streets for play. They checked a quarter mile radius around playgrounds in many cities under a wide range of conditions and found that only one seventh of the child population aged 5 to 15 was found on these grounds. They noted: "The lure of the street is a strong competitor ... The playground must be a well designed to compete successfully with the city streets, teeming with life and adventure" (cited in Jane Jacobs p.84-85). The folly of planning parks to lure children off the street is that parks can never compete with the stimuli offered by the street. The street is where real life happens. Parks can only ever hope to offer a pale imitation.

School of life: Christopher Alexander contends that "adults transmit their ethos and way of life to children through their actions, not through statements. Children learn by doing and copying" (p.294). There was a time when the whole city was an open book to children. They could skip into the butcher shop and chat to the butcher as he carved the meat. They could wander through the markets and back lanes. This was a time when "every child could gain experience (every day and near home) of what work, school, shopping, playing, fighting, being together, living and dying really mean. This was experience of the richness of human experience — or as Tellegan called it: 'the wholeness of life'" (Jan Tanghe et al p.166). The separation of the adult world from the child's world is a peculiar modern invention. As Christopher Alexander comments, it is unknown among animals and unknown in traditional cultures.

School of citizenship: Street play provided invaluable lessons in citizenship: the sharing of a space with other people and cooperatively turning it into a place of shared meanings. In play, children take the blank canvas of some space and, through innovation and negotiation with each other, transform this space into "a place". An hour later they renegotiate and give the same space some other meaning. Informal or spontaneous play is therefore the training ground for good citizenship: it teaches cooperation with others who are different from them to create a place of shared meaning. In fact, this informal play is training in "place making." These children will one day be in control

Nurenburg: A canvas on the road and some building blocks make an instant play area.

of shaping our cities. Their ability to transform barren spaces into places which are rich in meaning will depend on the skills they learnt as children of transforming a piece of sidewalk or asphalt into an exciting place.

The alternative to spontaneous street play is being driven to an organized sporting event. Here children interact with their peers in an event where the rules are made by someone else and enforced by an authority figure. The game emphasizes competition and individual performance rather than cooperation. While there are other values associated with this kind of planned event, the valuable citizenship and place-making lessons are missing. It is also poor training in the democratic processes of shared responsibility for society's collective life. It may not be stretching things too far to argue that if not balanced with spontaneous street play, the organised play prepares children better for totalitarian forms of relationships and governance rather than for cooperation and participatory democracy.

The lessons in citizenship taught through street play ran deeper than just the sharing and shaping of a common space. The adults who took some responsibility for supervising their play also modelled good citizenship. Children learnt that their freedom to use the streets came as the result of people extending themselves beyond their own individual concerns.

Sense of place: For millennia, the connection between people and the earth beneath their feet has been considered sacred. It provides "grounding" — an anchor. Street play was the first step in children being able to explore the territory around their home in ever increasing circles. This territory was gradually integrated into their home territory. In a sense, this gradual expansion of their home territory was a metaphor for the great adventure of life — the exploration of new paths and their integration into one's internal world.

Trans-generational interactions: Finally, by removing children from the street, we not only cut children off from the adult world, but we take away the opportunity for adults to interact with children.

We adults are apt to get wrapped up in our rational world. We forget that the irrational world of play and fantasy is the creative life-force of the universe. Being exposed to children's play in the course of our everyday activities is

Traffic restricts children's movement and therefore their ability to participate in city life.

essential in maintaining our sense of wonder, curiosity, adventure, and innocence — the qualities that make children inherently creative. To segregate the world of children's play from the serious world of adult work is to cut the adult world off from the source of its creativity.

How traffic erodes the tradition of children's street play

In just a few decades a belief has emerged that streets are for cars and that children have no right to use this space for play. To compound this, most homes now have a television which tries to replicate the drama and education that once took place on the street. This has placed us in another one of those vicious circles. In research undertaken by Hillman and others, the degree of freedom children have for independent mobility in the UK was measured. In 1971, 68% of 9-year-old children were allowed to visit leisure places alone. By 1990 this had fallen to just 37%. In 1971, 88% of 9-year-olds were allowed to go to school unaccompanied. In 1990 this was just 27% (cited in Tranter p.6). The reasons for this decrease are twofold. The chauffeuring of children to school or to leisure places increases the levels of traffic on the roads. Other parents respond to this by saying that the roads have become too dangerous to let their children walk. They too begin to chauffeur their children. (One third of all travel by females in the UK is now for the purpose of chauffeuring.) Secondly, because there are fewer people walking or cycling on the streets, perceptions of stranger danger increase, forcing parents either to chauffeur their children or to curtail their freedom of movement.

The act of chauffeuring children from one activity to another fractures the relationship children once established with the physical environment and the "earth," resulting in increasing feelings of insecurity and alienation.

It is interesting to note that in less economically wealthy parts of large cities, children still play in the streets. This is partly due to lack of private play spaces and lack of transport to take children to segregated play spaces. We are apt to look at these children and think they are 'deprived'. I re-

The increased freedom of the auto-age has been won at the expense of our children.

member watching the street life of a black neighborhood in Washington. Some children were playing basketball, using an old milk create wired to a garage door. People were sitting on front steps or standing at the front gate chatting. This was a neighborhood I had been advised not to enter. Yet for me, this neighborhood interaction seemed inherently healthy and desirable.

Looking to the future

Children are the future being shaped in the present. If our children are to build sustainable cities, they need placemaking and citizenship skills. There is no point trying to teach these skills in a classroom. These are skills that can only be developed through real-world practice and experimentation. While some of these skills can be developed in playgrounds, the playground is divorced from the adult world and the day-to-day activities of the city. Playgrounds can never replicate the authenticity of the placemaking and citizenship skills learnt in the street.

While segregating children's play from the everyday life of the city robs children of valuable education, it also sends a covert message that childhood and play are not part of the serious activity of the adult world. This downgrades the whole value of play in society. This covert message trains children to cut themselves off from their inherent creativity as they graduate from childhood to adulthood.

The reclaiming of our streets for children's play is therefore essential if we are to produce adults who are to be good stewards of our cities and the entire earth.

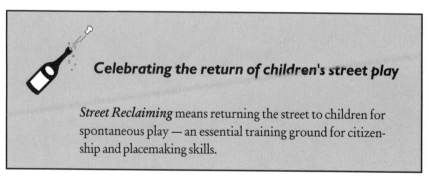

Celebrating the return of children's street play

Street Reclaiming means returning the street to children for spontaneous play — an essential training ground for citizenship and placemaking skills.

The Loss and Return of Street Wisdom

In the Jewish book of wisdom, collected some 3,000 years ago, it says in the introduction:

> Wisdom calls aloud in the street,
> she raises her voice in the public squares;
> at the head of the noisy streets she cries out,
> in the gateways of the city she makes her speech.

(Proverbs 1:20,21)

There is a long tradition of seeing the street as the place of wisdom. This tradition is preserved for us in the term "street wisdom." Why has the street been seen as a place of wisdom?

First we need to understand the concept of wisdom. Wisdom is not knowledge. Wisdom is knowing when and how to apply knowledge. Wisdom is a deeply creative act in that it finds a balance between paradoxes that put us on the horns of a dilemma. Should we show mercy or demand justice? Is it a time to build up or tear down? These dilemmas are not ones that can be solved with some off-the-shelf solution. Every situation is unique and can change from moment to moment. As the book of Jewish wisdom says, "To everything there is a season ... a time for peace and a time for war ... a time to plant and a time to reap." Wisdom discerns the season. Wisdom helps us walk the tightrope between paradoxical dilemmas. The Greeks had a view that through exposure to difficulty and diversity an individual would gradually attain *sophrosyne* — translated today as "grace" or "poise." Such a person was balanced or centred. *Sophrosyne* is the wisdom born of experience and pain. It is the ability to find exactly the right balance between those paradoxical pulls which place us in a dilemma.

In traditional societies the elders — those considered most wise — would sit at the city gate or in the city square and dispense their wisdom. Those with disputes would come to have them settled. Those caught in some deep dilemma would come to find a way through it. But street wisdom was not just the wisdom possessed by the elderly. It was the wisdom contained in the laughter and play of children. It was the wisdom contained in the jibes of the jester. It was the wisdom contained in the poems, songs, and paintings of the artists. It was the wisdom inherent in the pain of those who have been marginalized through ethnic origin or disabilities. The reason all these were seen as agents of wisdom is that each carried within a world of experience that was different to the world of experience of those seeking wisdom. By being exposed to this world of difference, the seekers of wisdom would become more balanced and better able to negotiate their internal dilemma.

Traditionally, the street was the place where those who possessed street wisdom would sit and share their wisdom with those who passed by.

The importance of the tradition of street wisdom

This tradition gave the elderly and those on the margin of society a vital role to play: they were the purveyors of wisdom. The commodity they gave freely was more valued than knowledge for it had to do with the art of living. This tradition allowed the elderly to take the role of mentors and nurturers of the entire community.

But why was their wisdom dispensed in the street? Because their wisdom was a gift to the *entire* community. It was public property just as the street itself was public property. And perhaps we should not underestimate the power of the symbolism. Streets are symbolic of a journey. The elderly, having undertaken the journey, sit in the street to give guidance and direction to those travellers standing at the crossroads deciding which way to go.

If streets are symbolic of a journey from one destination to another, then they are also symbolic of the journey of life from birth to death. This symbolism was given poignant meaning in the traditional city by having the young play in the streets, often watched over by the very old. This gave to life a sense of rhythm and wholeness.

How traffic erodes the tradition of street wisdom

The street is no longer seen as a place for the elderly or marginalized to dispense their wisdom. Instead it has become the sole province of machines. To add insult to injury, we warehouse our elderly while they await death.

How could we, as a society, so callously strip the elderly and marginalized of the vital role they have played for millennia? The seeds of this development go back to the birth of the scientific movement. We began to view the universe and ourselves in machine terms. We became preoccupied with efficiency and the material products produced by the machine. Suddenly human life took on three distinct stages: childhood in which we trained to be a productive adult; adulthood where we produced things of value and consumed these commodities; and old-age where the productive machine had worn out and was replaced by the more productive machines that were graduating from childhood.

In such a society, cars are highly valued, for they promise to increase the efficiency and productivity of the adult producer. Wedded to their car, adult producers can do more things in a shorter time. (As we shall discover later, this became a tragic illusion when too many adults tried to increase their productivity through using their car.) Streets also took on a narrow machine function, their value being the efficiency with which they could move productive adults in their vehicles.

It is therefore no accident that we have segregated the world of the child, the elderly, and the marginalized from the everyday world of the city. We no longer see the city as the crucible for evolving more noble life. It is a machine for producing consumer goods, and we are cogs in that machine. Children, the elderly, and the marginalized are not productive cogs.

This segregation of life into three distinct phases has dire psychological consequences for us all, but particularly for the elderly. Not only do the elderly feel useless because they are no longer "producers," but the one valuable gift they have to give to the wider community is shunned. Their childhood and maturing process is torn away from their old age.

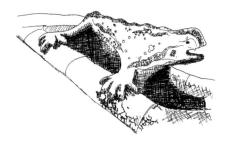

Looking to the future

While this may paint a very bleak picture, it describes *one* way of thinking — a value framework that has gained too much power. Thankfully there is a another way of thinking which is beginning to assert its authority and thus to restore a better balance. Within our civilization runs a very deep and powerful tradition which celebrates our "humanity." Street reclaiming is really about reclaiming our humanness — and in particular about reintegrating the world of the child, the elderly, and the marginalized back into everyday life.

If our society has become dehumanized (and many would argue that it has), then the antidote is to stop viewing ourselves as machines and to look at the world through the eyes of the elderly, the marginalized, those with disabilities, children, jesters, and artists.

Knowledge is the fodder that feeds the machine age. Knowledge can produce better machines, or help us live longer. But it is useless in helping us create a more civilized and compassionate society. For that we need wisdom. And wisdom resides in that portion of the population which the machine age considers unproductive.

Our society awaits a social revolution that parallels the revolution which has taken place in relationship to the natural environment. Until recently we considered swamps and marshlands as "wastelands" — a waste of land. They seemed to serve no productive purpose. Then we discovered that these wastelands contained great pools of bio-diversity which were in fact our life-link to the future. Socially, the pools of socio-diversity reside within the life-experience of those on the margin of society. We have to stop seeing them as a "waste of space" and to learn to value them as our life-link to the future. As we shall see later, the chief place that we can be exposed to their wisdom is still the street.

Reclaiming our streets as a place for the exchange of wisdom is a way of integrating the elderly and those on the margin into community life. If we do so, we will be giving a gift to ourselves. For we too will grow old.

Celebrating the return of street wisdom

Street Reclaiming is taking back the street as a place for the elderly and those on the margin of society to share their street wisdom.

The Loss and Return of Adult Play Space

Streets were not just play space for children — they were also play space for adults.

As Robert Banks shows in *The Tyranny of Time*, we have the illusion that we live in the "leisure age." While factory workers worked 60 hours per week 100 years ago, this was a brief aberration in history. In the Middle Ages and even in Classical Antiquity, the number of holy days — or holidays — was about 115 a year. In addition, workers in many occupations had additional days off depending on the seasons and the weather. The streets were the traditional setting for the festivities that accompanied these holy days.

Today, if one visits some European cities, this tradition of streets being a place for adult play is still alive. Recently I witnessed the twilight activities in the streets and parks of Barcelona. Some people were happy to sit on benches and chat. Simultaneously, one adult was teaching his friend to ride a unicycle. Others watched and then joined in. This adult play was surrounded by children's play — teenagers playing table tennis on an outdoor table, kids playing soccer or riding their bikes.

Another form of adult play practised in many European and South American cultures is the promenade. Adults play "dress ups" while those who sit and watch get

Seats at this outdoor cafe in Paris are arranged to deliberately encourage "people watching" — a form of adult play in which we make up stories about others.

Our entire civilization was conceived in play and fantasy. And play and fantasy remain its life-blood. They are our link to the future.

to make up stories in their heads about those who have dressed up. These storytellers or people-watchers study the clothes of those who promenade, their mannerisms, their companions, and their body language, and from these clues, create a story about the person. These stories may be simple one-act plays on the theme of, "How on earth did she end up with him," or much longer sagas. In many cities around the world, seats are deliberately arranged in ways to encourage promenading and people watching.

The organic street layout of older cities with their large "living rooms" provides a wonderful stage for all kinds of street drama. Around many of these street rooms or outdoor stages, the buildings even feature viewing boxes from which occupants can watch the drama played out below.

Today, in North American, British, and Australian culture, this tradition of the street as a place for adult play is preserved in street festivals, mardi gras parades, and lantern processions. On these special occasions we ban traffic from the street and turn them over to celebration.

The importance of the tradition of adult street play

It is difficult in our current cultural setting, with its strong work ethic, to imagine that some cultures viewed adult play as an essential part of a civilized society. Lewis Mumford, quoting Dutch historian J. Huizinga, contends that play rather than work is the formative element in human culture and that humanity's most serious activity belongs to the realm of make-believe. Mumford then traces human development, arguing that the dream was the source of all the arts and of our entire civilization. From the dream, early humans discovered two connected qualities of the emerging mind. The imaginary worlds created in their dreams could be constructed during waking hours by the conscious mind. From this developed the capacity for "storytelling" — the ability consciously to construct fantasy worlds. We can imagine that even before language was developed humans found that they could impersonate each other and that this resulted in a rather nice body reaction: laughter. It would not be long before the impersonation became exaggerated and extended in order to increase this amusement. With mimicking of animals added, humans had a fully developed storytelling capacity even before language was invented. They had the ability to consciously create make-believe worlds, to communicate these, and to trigger emotions in those watching or participating.

This ability to create fantasy worlds allowed the developing humans to explore realms beyond immediate reality. Every tool they created and every new technology was first created in their imagination. This is why play and fantasy were foundational to the whole development of civilization.

Interestingly enough, it is through play and fantasy that children build their adult identity, thus mirroring our evolution as a species. Through play and fantasy children try on various roles for themselves like play-clothes. Some they discard. Others they adopt.

For the adult, there can be no creation without returning to the world of the child, a world dominated by play and fantasy. But play and fantasy do more than enrich our creative abilities. They are essential to our spiritual and emotional well-being. For example, in people-watching the stories we create about other people are not really stories about other people. They are stories about ourselves, stories constructed from the fragments of our own life experience.

If, for example, we pass a small child that is crying, the story we construct for that child is one that reflects the painful events of our own childhood. People-watching is therefore a process of holding a mirror to our own inner self. By having the fragments of our own past resurrected from the dark cellars of our memory, we are presented with the opportunity of reinventing our past by weaving its fragments into a new story.

However, people-watching is also a way of inventing our future. If it is an older person we see, then we are confronted with our own mortality. We are forced to think about what we will have achieved by the time we reach their old age. Like children's play, people-watching is an act of play-acting in which we get to try out future roles for ourselves.

But it is not just the presence of others in the street which evokes the storyteller and playful child within. In the traditional street there were music, water, art, festivals, clowns, eccentrics, children, absurdity, lovers, and chaos. These feed the inherent creativity of the human brain. Science tells us that there are particular environmental conditions under which nature is most prolific in creating new life forms. They are the same conditions under which the human brain is most creative. We need a diversity of stimuli and a "mixing bowl" for the stimuli. The diversity of the street,

Play is a relationship with reality which is not in the first place decided by the necessities of life, is not trapped with any financial or productivity relationships, but which finds its interest and fulfilment within itself. It is an open relationship with reality: creativity and spontaneity. Experience gained in play is decisive for awareness later on, for the pattern of one's reactions and the capacity to deal with the unknown. The serious world of grown-ups — where "everything must be done" is put in perspective in play.

Jan Tanghe et al., *Living Cities*

together with its inherent chaos and ambiguity, forces the human brain to create order where none exists. To do this, we must invent stories which give the universe, our cities, our streets, and our lives meaning.

How traffic erodes the tradition of adult street play

Traffic has eroded the ability for people-watching and playful activities. Instead we have turned inward to a mechanized forms of play and people-watching: the television. Instead of creating our own fantasy plots, we allow others to do it for us. In addition, there has been the cultural shift explored earlier where we view ourselves largely as machines. Play, fantasy, and celebration are seen as nonproductive — luxuries we can only indulge in when the "real" work is done. In this world, traffic (containing people doing "real" work) must take precedence over adults and children who are "only" playing. It is just on special occasions that we are allowed to close the street to traffic and have an organised festival or parade. Even these events tend to be controlled, leaving little room for exuberant, uninhibited adult play.

Looking to the future

Adult play is the engine-room of our current civilization. If the loss of adult play space is taken to an extreme, it will threaten the sustainability of our entire civilisation. Play is the only means we have of exploring new destinations. Without it we are in a rudderless ship at the mercy of whatever storms the universe may throw our way. With play we can harness the storms to drive us to new and exciting destinations.

In play, animals, people or whole societies get to experiment with all sorts of combinations and permutations ... that would not be possible in a world that functions on immediate survival values. A creature that plays is more readily adaptable to changing contexts and conditions. Play as free improvisation sharpens our capacity to deal with a changing world.

Stephen Nachmanovitch, *Free Play*

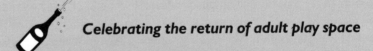

Celebrating the return of adult play space

Street Reclaiming means reclaiming the street for adult play: people-watching, promenading, water, art, celebration, festivals, eating, or just hanging out.

The Loss and Return of the Local Economy

Earlier I argued that cities are an invention to concentrate exchange opportunities and to minimize travel. This concentration of exchange opportunities includes the commercial exchange of goods, skills, and services. The city is therefore an invention to minimize the costs of these commercial exchanges by reducing the costs associated with transport. The closer the proximity of raw materials, workers and markets the smaller the costs associated with transport.

Historically, this led to a very strong local economy with a wide diversity and density of commercial exchange opportunities close to where people lived. This meant that streets were not just used for transporting raw materials, workers, goods, and customers. They were a hotbed of economic activity with street vendors, farmers' markets, craft stalls, traveling salespeople, and home deliveries. Even cities like Brisbane with its suburban sprawl saw plenty of economic activity in residential streets. As one old-timer told me:

> We would all go out to the butcher's cart and he would carve up the meat
> right there in the street. While the butcher was cutting up the meat, we'd all
> stand around chatting and then someone would ask everyone back to their
> house for a cup of tea.

Another old-timer remembers how important these economic activities were as a social event, even for children:

> Yes, as a kid we used to have open run and follow the baker's cart around and
> sit on the back and have a free ride. And if you had sixpence, you bought a few
> cakes off the cake man. I remember the fruiter coming around and that was a
> big event down the street. He always sang out to us and we used to ask for a
> few specks to help our family get by ....

The importance of the tradition of local commerce

Using the street as a place of commerce provided room for new enterprises to start up. One did not have to rent a high-priced shop in a large regional shopping mall or business park. Some businesses could start rent-free right in the street. Others could find very low rents in the older buildings that formed part of the street fabric. The hubbub of economic activity already happening in the street increased the chances of these new businesses growing and moving into more permanent facilities. This provided a greater diversity of businesses — and by extension a greater diversity of goods and services — than do economies that are centralized. The bottom line was that as a result of the concentration of exchange opportunities (which reduced transport costs) the price of goods and services became cheaper.

How traffic erodes the tradition of local commerce

As we have already discussed, traffic dilutes the density of exchange opportunities and scatters them wider, thereby reducing the efficiency with which they can be transacted. Just by virtue of its space demands, traffic erodes the viability of the local economy.

However, there is another factor which has sped up this slow strangling of the local economy: subsidizing businesses to centralize. Industry has been allowed to consolidate small local facilities into larger regional facilities, arguing that these provide economies of scale. In reality, we subsidize industry by creating these large regional facilities. The first subsidy is in the area of transport costs. Instead of industry paying to bring the goods virtually to our back door, they bring the goods half way and we transport them the rest of the way. This involves not just the immediate gasoline costs of transporting the goods by car, but the entire costs of needing a car in the first place. However, the greatest subsidy involves the way creating these larger regional facilities has imposed "second generation costs" on the whole of society. Roads must be provided or widened to get cars to the large regional facility. This automatically results in urban sprawl. It requires a greater level of infrastructure to serve the same number of people — more roads, electricity, water mains, sewerage, and drainage.

This imposes ongoing costs on all citizens for running and maintaining this dispersed infrastructure. Then there are the increased transport costs, not just for getting to the shopping centre, but for getting to *everything:* work, school, friends, entertainment, etc.

Add to these infrastructure and transport costs the costs associated with neighborhood fragmentation. Loss of the local economy means a loss of social contact. To compound the problem, the extra traffic generated by centralized facilities erodes the social fabric of everyone's neighborhood. What costs are we paying as a society for this increasing sense of alienation — particularly with our children?

Because these costs of moving from a local economy to a regional economy are not transparent to either the entrepreneur or the customer, we can live with the illusion that large regional facilities provide cheaper goods than local facilities.

But there is also another cost which is often overlooked. Let us compare a product produced and sold locally and selling for $10 with the same product which sells for $8 but was mass produced in a centralized location, then transported over vast distances to a centralized distribution centre to which you must drive to pick it up. With the product produced and sold locally, let us imagine that $2 go to materials, $2 to transport of raw materials, $2 to labor to produce the product, $2 to salaries for sales staff, and $2 to the proprietor as profit. Out of the $10 purchase price, at least $6 ($2 labor, $2 salaries, and $2 profit to proprietor) stay in the local economy to be spent on other goods and services. With the product produced and sold regionally, $2 may go to materials, $3 to transport, $1 to production labor (higher levels of mechanization or off-shore-production), $1 to salaries (cut in service level), and $1 to the proprietor as profit. Out of the $8 you spend on this product, at best $3 may stay in the local economy — less if the proprietor is a large corporate chain with headquarters in some other city or country. The $2 you saved are then eaten up by burning fuel to access the goods and by the ongoing costs of a scattered and inefficient city. Spending a higher percentage of your disposable income on other people's labor and less on transport costs puts more money in the local economy, which is to ultimately buy yourself a job.

Looking to the future

In many industrialised countries unemployment is unacceptably high — particularly youth unemployment. The problem, as I see it, is this. Our economy is built on an ever increasing consumption of goods. However, the production of these goods requires less and less labor as manufacturing is automated or moved off shore to "developing" countries. Government programs are often aimed simply at helping the growing pool of unemployed to be more sophisticated in the way they compete for this dwindling supply of jobs.

Access to meaningful employment is a human right and should be a central feature of any civilized city. If we are to build sustainable cities — cities that are sustainable both ecologically and socially — then the whole issue of how we structure the economy of the city is central. Such an economy cannot be based on ever increasing consumption, the burning of non-renewable resources, and dwindling labor content in the production of goods. It must be based on quality, not on quantity. One measure of quality is the degree of local labor present in the product.

A strong local economy requires the return of the street as a venue for commerce. We need to consider the many ways this can be done. In Chapter Three I show how many residential streets could include corner stores, coffee shops, home-delivery depots, or telecommute facilities (a grander version of the internet cafe where workstations could be rented for as long as necessary). I also suggest ad-hoc commercial ventures like weekend farmers' markets or artesian markets. I acknowledge that many neighborhoods will resist changing their mono-cultural street environment. But others will understand the social, cultural, and economic benefits of creating more diverse and efficient neighborhoods. In addition, local shopping centres need to allow street merchants. The reaction by some established merchants may be that this will take business away from them. But the contrary will happen. The increased choices will attract more customers and the local streets will exhibit more colour, diversity, and activity, turning the shopping trip into a social and cultural outing.

Celebrating the return of the local economy
Street Reclaiming means rebuilding the local economy as the engine-room of the city economy and a primary wealth generator.

The Loss and Return of a More Democratic Community

Streets and public squares were the birthplace of democracy. As Grady Clay noted: "In nineteenth-century novels and plays, the street epitomized democracy-in-action. It stood for an open society with freedom of access at its very core and foundation" (Roberta Brandes Gratz, p.296).

However, the tradition goes even further back. The Greek word for "city" was "civitas" meaning a collection of citizens. The city was a "collective enterprise" and the street was the lifeblood of this collaborative effort. Aristotle equated exchange with the bonds of community. If there is exchange, he wrote, there is a community; and there is no community without exchange. The street was the place of equality in exchange. Tony Hiss comments:

> As each Athenian went about his business, both public and private — going to the gymnasium, the theatre, and the marketplace; climbing up the Acropolis and walking down to the harbour; attending annual city-wide concerts and festivals of singing and dancing; and serving on juries, and in the assembly, and also in the military — the citizen was exposed to experiences that together and cumulatively produced, as Mumford said, "not a new type of city, but a new type of man... For a while, city and citizen were one" (xviii).

The street is the marketplace of ideas, including political ideas. The street has always been viewed as the bastion of free speech. Symbolically, we still see the street march as a basic right of protest in a democracy. Dictators and authoritarian governments usually begin their suppression of free speech by controlling street activity. In the 1860's, Napoleon the Third was concerned about potential political uprisings in the slums of Paris with their mazes of narrow streets. His answer was to instruct Baron Haussmann to carve boulevards through these slum areas so that troops could get in and quell any uprisings.

The importance of the tradition of a democratic community

In any society there are marginalized groups, people who are not at the centre of action. These may be senior citizens, eccentrics, children, people with intellectual or physical disabilities, women, ethnic groups, etc. Because these people are "on the margin," their experience of life is very different to that

We need places where friends may stroll, but where they share the same social space with people outside their set, a space that is owned equally by many kinds of people. Without such spaces for the normalization of diversity, a society becomes brittle, unadaptable, fragmented, calcified, and weak.

Mike Greenberg, *The Poetics of Cities*

of those at the centre of the action. These people on the margins, with their different life experience, represent the socio-diversity of a society. It is this pool of diversity which feeds the creative life of the city and from which new life forms will emerge to meet the challenges of a changing world. The Greeks were therefore right in believing that the greatness of any civilization would be judged by how well they integrated those on the margin into mainstream community life.

So how do those on the margin get to contribute their invaluable gifts to society? Or, to change the question, how does mainstream society access this diversity of life experience held in store by those on the margins? Almost exclusively through spontaneous encounters. We don't plan to go and have an exchange with the eccentric that sits on a milk crate outside the corner store playing his tin whistle. We pass him on our way to get the milk and nod. Then one day we say hello. Then one day we stop and hold a conversation and in the conversation we become exposed to his inner world

Towns, where we become citizens and can be seen, begin directly outside our door, where the road stands for public life. If, as the Greeks believed, the gods in their wandering made the first roads, then I daresay it is an act of piety to follow in their footsteps, and politically speaking, the best of all landscapes, the best of all roads, are those which foster a movement toward a desirable social goal.

John Brinckerhoff Jackson, *Discovering the Vernacular Landscape*

The greatness of any city can be judged by how well it integrates those on the margins into community life.

which is so different to ours. To destroy the spontaneous encounter realm of the city is therefore to rob ourselves and the city of the contribution these people on the margin have to make. Or, put another way, the spontaneous encounter realm is the chief mechanism that those on the margin have for making their contribution to city life. Take away the corner store and you take away the "stage" for the eccentric with the tin whistle. Take away the customers walking to the corner store and you take away the eccentric's audience.

It is interesting that in the traditional city, it was this spontaneous exchange which provided the support mechanisms for those on the margin. The eccentric with the tin whistle would be "owned" by the entire neighborhood. People would discover the needs of those on the margin through conversation. Their sense of citizenship and compassion would compel them to meet those needs — to accompany them to the doctor, to buy them a coffee, to give them a pair of shoes. Thus was established a relationship of mutual benefit.

How traffic erodes the tradition of a democratic community

Earlier I contended that traffic erodes the spontaneous exchange. I have just argued that the spontaneous exchange realm is the chief mechanism supporting the active participation of those at the margins of community life. In a city which has moved increasingly to planned exchanges, the informal local support mechanisms for those at the margins are eroded and there is an increasing reliance on formal support mechanisms: government agencies or charitable organisations. Help and aid become depersonalized, undermining a sense of identity for both those on the margin and those who once offered help. Combine this with the weakening of the local economy, and those on the margin have a sense that their role in society — as the ears and the eyes of the street — has been downgraded or totally eliminated.

Looking to the future

Reducing opportunities for spontaneous exchange downgrades the ability of those on the margin to participate meaningfully in community life. Allowing traffic to convert the dual functions of the street — a place for movement and a place for exchange — into a single function is to alienate even further those on the margin and to remove their voice from the democratic process. Ultimately this is an attack on our own future. Sooner or later we will all join the ranks of those on the margin. As a person with paraplegia reminded me one day: "There is an old person or disabled person in everyone of us just waiting to get out."

In classical Greece, one wasn't considered a complete person unless one were part of a polis; *the definition of citizen was tied to the notion of city, community, and shared responsibility. Banishment from the city was therefore the ultimate punishment. In a sense, modern industrial culture has banished most of us from that essential connection with our environment, community, and our* polis. *Our future lies in reestablishing those links.*

Sim Van der Ryn and Peter Calthorpe, *Sustainable Communities*

Streets and the spontaneous encounter realm are the cornerstones of Western democracy. Planned exchanges can be controlled. But the spontaneous realm is an open forum for debate, for a sharing of ideas and insights. The reduction of the spontaneous encounter realm in the city therefore undermines the ability of all citizens to participate in the democratic process. The greater the controls we see over public space (including streets) the more repressive and totalitarian the political system.

If we are to create more compassionate and civilized cities, we must look back to the roots of the city. The word "politics" is derived from "polis" — the city. The city gave rise to a new vision of governance — a vision of the city as a collective enterprise in which each person took on the responsibility of citizenship.

For the past few decades, our society has emphasized the values of competition and the rights of the individual. But if we are to build compassionate and civilized cities, these values need to be balanced with a vision of cooperation and the duties of citizenship. This requires the return of the street as the central stage for the democratic process.

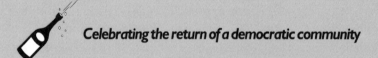

Celebrating the return of a democratic community

Street Reclaiming means reclaiming the street as the stage upon which those at the margin of society can make a contribution to community life. A vibrant street life is essential for any egalitarian, democratic society and central to a healthy political process.

chapter two

CUTTING TRAFFIC BY HALF

The Five R's of Traffic Reduction

Traffic Reduction: As Easy as Recycling Trash

From Chapter One it is obvious that in order to reclaim our streets and city, we need to reduce dramatically traffic volume and speed. This will allow us

- to restore the dual functions of the street as a place for both movement and social, cultural, and economic exchange, and
- to convert some of the space that is saved, both road and parking space, back into exchange spaces that will enhance the quality of life of residents.

In the past it has been believed that reducing overall traffic levels in the city is not a viable option. It is assumed that current levels of traffic are a given that we must accept. However, reducing traffic is as simple as recycling trash (rubbish). This chapter shows how traffic can be cut in half — without anyone forgoing a single thing.

The connection between trash and traffic

The connection between trash reduction and traffic reduction emerged from some work I did for Brisbane City Council in 1994. I had been commissioned to look for solutions to traffic problems in Fortitude Valley, an inner-city location drowning in traffic. In a workshop with the community I was explaining how transport planners and the community at large were making a huge assumption about traffic. We all believed that current levels of traffic were a given that simply had to be accommodated.

To illustrate my point, I asked them to remember back 10–15 years when almost every council in the world assumed that the amount of trash in the waste stream was a given and that cities simply had to find bigger and better landfill sites. Suddenly, as landfill sites began to run out, Councils like that in Brisbane began to examine the waste stream more carefully and discovered that 80% of the trash didn't need to go to landfill sites at all. Using resource management techniques — the 3R's of trash reduction — these Councils set ambitious reduction targets, in the case of Brisbane a 50% reduction within 8 years. Almost overnight, recycling moved from a fringe environmentalists' activity to mainstream culture.

I explained to the meeting that we are in the same position with traffic as we were with trash 10–15 years ago. It is assumed that all of the traffic on the roads needs to be there and that this requires bigger and better roads. No one has bothered to examine the traffic stream to see what percentage doesn't really need to be there.

Over coffee, residents talked excitedly about how helpful the trash analogy

The prime objective of sustainable urban planning is to reduce significantly the kilometres per capita covered every day to get to work, school, home, or recreational facilities. Ideally, the citizen who walks could accomplish all his daily functions — without the aid of mechanised transport — in a maximum of ten minutes.

Salvador Rueda et. al., *The Sustainable City*

had been. One of the residents gave me a lift home and we continued to chat about the connection between trash reduction and traffic reduction. Suddenly it struck me that the connection was not just metaphorical. Car trips *are* packaging — a "waste" we produce in getting access to "products." These products may be coffee and a chat with a friend, work, education, shopping, etc. There is no value in the car trip itself — unless it is a Sunday drive in the country or the prestige we get by driving a particular brand of car. The real value of the car is in what it gives us access to. Just as a bread wrapper is a waste we produce in gaining access to bread, car trips produce a broad range of "waste" in giving us access to particular products. These wastes include air and water pollution; the destruction of natural environments and farmlands consumed by the extra space demands of the car; money spent on running our vehicle and on servicing the infrastructure needed to run the vehicle; our time, particularly when congestion imposes time delays on everyone.

As we chatted, it dawned on me that you could use the same 3 R's of trash reduction to reduce car use (later I expanded them to the 5 R's of Traffic Reduction.)

Cutting traffic by Half

In the report I wrote for Brisbane City Council, I did some theoretical projections based on a broad range of research. I suggested that peak-hour traffic could be reduced by 57% just by eliminating some of the current inefficiencies in the system. For

Cars trips are 'packaging' — a price we pay to get access to goods and services.

example, I looked at occupancy rates (number of people in each car) and found that in the previous ten years, occupancy rates had fallen by 12% — down to just 1.17 persons per car. By going back to the occupancy rates we had ten years previously, we could reduce peak-hour traffic by 12%. I looked at cross commuting — an inefficient arrangement where, for example, a school teacher from suburb A teaches in suburb Z and a school teacher from suburb Z teaches in suburb A and they pass each other on the freeway each morning and night. Australian researchers found that eliminating this inefficient arrangement would reduce traffic by 60%. I suggested that by establishing a "work and employ locally campaign" and a job exchange bureau, we could aim for a modest target of 8% reduction in cross-commuting over the next ten years — less than 1% per year. Research also indicated that telecommuting (working from home via computer) could reduce peak-hour traffic by 35%, with indications that this figure would grow significantly in the next decade. I suggested we aim for a 1% reduction per year over the next ten years, which would contribute an overall 10% reduction in peak-hour traffic. Research also suggested that land-use changes (creating integrated local area environments with balanced residences, employment, services, and public transport) could slash average journey lengths by 50%. I suggested an overall goal of 10% over the next ten years. I recommended that of the trips that remained, 7% could be switched to public transport, 2% to walking and 5% to cycling. As a result of the small gains from all these inefficiencies, peak hour traffic could be reduced by 57%.

In the year that followed, I developed the *Car Activity Diary* (see p. 62) as a means of seeing how much people could reduce their car use without foregoing anything. (Trash reduction does not ask people to eat less. It asks them to reduce the waste they produce while improving their quality of life.) The diary exercise got people to list the stops they had made in their car the previous day. The stops were important because at each stop they gained access to a particular "product." The *Car Activity Diary* then asked respondents to look at the 5 R's of Traffic Reduction to see how much they could have reduced the total number of kilometres/miles they had driven while still getting all the "products" they had accessed through their car.

The results were astounding. The first workshop in Brisbane (40 participants) found they could reduce their overall car use by 49% and peak-hour traffic by 57% (the fact that this figure is the same as the theoretical work I did for Brisbane City Council is a mere coincidence). The research was repeated in Vancouver (Canada) with a group of planners, bureaucrats, and concerned residents. They said they could reduce their overall car use by 80%.

The planners in Vancouver raised an interesting question. The figure of 80% represented a *potential* reduction. What was a *feasible* reduction?

There is no shared life in Loopland, no historical memory, no soil to sustain roots. It is a location to be occupied for a while and then abandoned without sentiment, turf to be guarded, not a garden to be husbanded. It's like a parking lot for lives.

Mike Greenberg, *The Poetics of Cities*

Well, theoretically the potential reduction is not 80% but 100%. For thousands of years cities did function relatively efficiently without private cars. If for health reasons we decided that cars had to be totally banned from our cities, we would cope. In fact, we would probably do much better than cope. We would invent efficient means of public transport that combined the current flexibility of the private car with the space efficiency and sociability of public transport. We would rediscover streets as the epicenter of community and cultural life.

However, this begs the question. What can we feasibly expect in the short and longer term? I explained to these planning professionals that trash again provided a useful model. Councils like that in Brisbane had found that an 80% reduction in the waste stream was possible. However, the ease with which these reductions could be accomplished is layered. The first 20% may be extremely easy. In Brisbane, there were already existing newspaper and aluminium recycling industries that could simply be expanded. The next 20-40% would be a little more difficult, requiring greater change. For example, to get people to compost their vegetable scraps and garden waste required making composting bins available, at cost, to all households. The last 20% of the 80% may be extremely difficult and require the invention of new technologies. I surmised that the potential savings from traffic reduction were also layered. To test this, I redesigned the Car Activity Diary, asking people to rank their potential savings into 1. Easy, and just my responsibility; 2. Moderately easy with a little help from government; 3. Difficult, but not impossible. This new format was tested with residents in both Vancouver and Ottawa. They reported that a 25–30% reduction was easy and just their responsibility; it required no support from council or government.

This result made me very excited. For years I had heard the same rhetoric in every city: "We cannot reduce car use until we have better public transport, bike ways and walking facilities." Others argued that higher density and mixed use (a wider range of facilities close to home) were needed. This created a chicken-and-egg problem. Residents argued that they could not reduce their car use until there was better public transport while government slashed services because of lack of patronage. The research results from Vancouver and Ottawa suggested a way to short-circuit this catch-22 situation. By starting with the reductions that are immediately available and do not require better public transport (or other forms of government intervention), one would create a momentum and support base for improving public transport which would encourage further reductions in car use. Eliminating the 25–30% inefficiency in existing transport choices, would provide the support and momentum for improving the transport

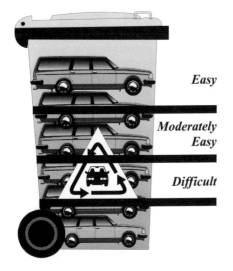

Easy

Moderately Easy

Difficult

The ease with which traffic can be reduced is layered, just as it is for waste reduction.

choices and landuse settings. In fact, there is strong evidence to suggest that in some cities, this potential first-level saving is as high as 50%. In the first trial of the *Traffic Reduction Kit* in Brisbane, residents produced a 34% reduction in their car use during a trial week. Even more striking is the evidence from Car Share Clubs in Europe. In 1997, these clubs operated in 250 cities with 20,000 members. Members do not own their own car but join a club that has a number of cars parked centrally in their neighborhood. Those members who sold their cars to join the clubs found that on average their car use dropped by 50% (measured in distance travelled). This can be attrib-

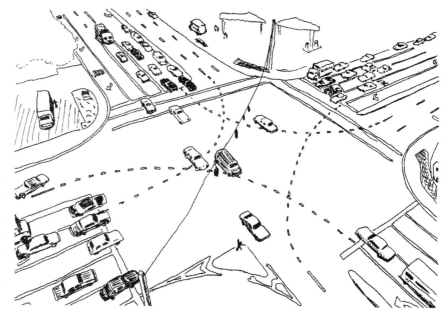

uted to the fact that they had real incentives to organize their car use more efficiently; they had to book the car, walk to a holding yard, and pay the "true" costs of every kilometre/mile they drove. Currently car owners are not aware of the true costs of their driving because many of the costs are paid in lump sums and then forgotten.

Before we examine each of the 5 R's of Traffic Reduction, it is important to dismiss a common myth. Most planners and city authorities equate traffic reduction with reducing the number of trips people make. However, using reduction in the number of trips as the measure of success can be very misleading. You can halve the number of trips in a city, but if each journey becomes twice as long, there is still exactly the same amount of traffic in the system. The only meaningful measure of traffic reduction is a reduction in the number of kilometres/miles vehicles are being driven — in technical terms, the vehicle kilometres/miles per person per year. While reducing the number of trips is one of the 5R's, all five reduction strategies have to be viewed as working together, not as goals in themselves.

The ultimate goal of Traffic Reduction is to reduce the total number of kilometres/miles people are driving in their cars...and by extension, the amount of space that these vehicles need.

Over: *The Car Activity Diary and summary of the 5 R's of Traffic Reduction.*

CAR ACTIVITY DIARY

GOAL: Reduce your car use while still doing everything you did!

INSTRUCTIONS:

1 Pick closest normal work day just past.
2 Select primary car you used.
3 List ALL the stops made in this vehicle during day. (See example bottom of page.)
4 Estimate distances between each stop.
5 Use household reduction strategies (opposite) to reduce your car use.
6 Work out Km saved (instructions opposite).
7 Determine whether reductions are easy, moderately easy or hard.
8 Calculate your savings.

Starting Point for day	YOUR CAR'S ACTIVITIES		WHAT YOU COULD HAVE SAVED		
	Purpose of this stop (e.g. buy bread). List ALL stops	Estimated distance from last stop	Household Reduction Strategy	Distance saved	Easy Moderately Easy or Hard to achieve?
Stop 1 •					
Stop 2 •					
Stop 3 •					
Stop 4 •					
Stop 5 •					
Stop 6 •					
Stop 7 •					
Stop 8 •					
Stop 9 •					
Stop 10 •					
Stop 10 •					
Stop 12 •					
Stop 13 •					
Stop 14 •					
Stop 15 •					
	Estimated Distance Travelled		**SAVED!!**		

Home	EXAMPLE				
Stop 1	John to School	1.5	Cycle (fix puncture)	1.5	Easy
Stop 2	Home	1.5	As above	1.5	Easy
Stop 3	Shop to buy milk	1	Home Delivery	1	Mod. Hard
Stop 4	Home	1	As above	1	Mod. Hard

▼ 5 R's of Traffic Reduction

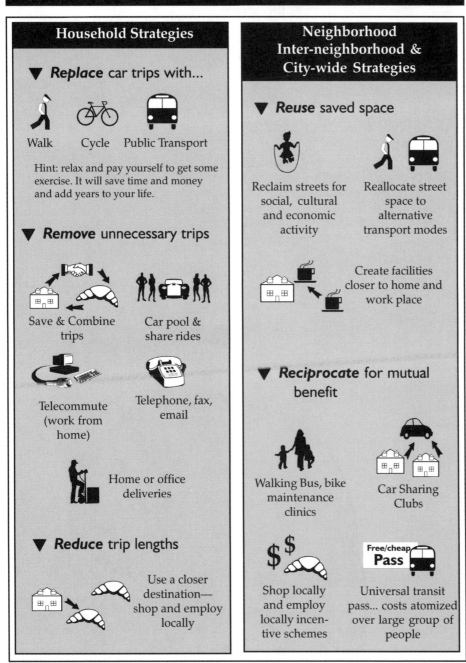

Household Strategies

▼ *Replace* car trips with...

Walk　　Cycle　　Public Transport

Hint: relax and pay yourself to get some exercise. It will save time and money and add years to your life.

▼ *Remove* unnecessary trips

Save & Combine trips

Car pool & share rides

Telecommute (work from home)

Telephone, fax, email

Home or office deliveries

▼ *Reduce* trip lengths

Use a closer destination— shop and employ locally

Neighborhood Inter-neighborhood & City-wide Strategies

▼ *Reuse* saved space

Reclaim streets for social, cultural and economic activity

Reallocate street space to alternative transport modes

Create facilities closer to home and work place

▼ *Reciprocate* for mutual benefit

Walking Bus, bike maintenance clinics

Car Sharing Clubs

Shop locally and employ locally incentive schemes

Universal transit pass... costs atomized over large group of people

Free/cheap **Pass**

How to Calculate Your Savings

The total distance is saved for all reduction strategies except the following:

Combine two or more trips
All the shortest legs are saved, longest leg is not saved.

Car pool or share ride
- •• If 2 people car pool you save 1/2 the journey length
- ••• 3 people -- 2/3
- •••• 4 people -- 3/4
- ••••• 5 people -- 4/5

Use closer destination
Saving is difference between the closer destination and the one further away.

The vehicle also turns its occupants into disadvantaged persons, for it distracts them from the very activities that make cities happen: the face to face exchange of goods, services, information, and ideas.

John Roberts, 8th Annual Pedestrian Conference

Walking, cycling, and using public transport allow us to meet a host of interesting people along the way.

The point about time and speed that our civilization has yet to understand is that both can annihilate experience, that is, rob experience of absorption, reflection, inner organization, reformulation of thought and behavior, and, ultimately, human meaning. Behavior that is rushed, rigidly paced or constantly pressed for greater output easily becomes barren of social worth or robbed of interpersonal feeling... The compulsive goer loses touch with the reason for going, the doer with the reason for doing.

Kenneth Schneider, *On The Nature of Cities*

Reduction Strategy 1: Replace Some Car Trips

The first of the 5R's of Traffic Reduction is to replace some trips with walking, cycling, or using public transport.

In the past, many people have seen using these modes of transport, particularly walking and cycling, as slow and inefficient compared to driving a car. But are they?

Traditionally, the only time considered when comparing the speed of walking or cycling to driving the car is the actual time spent travelling. But this ignores two other important time costs, the first being the time spent earning the money to pay the costs of buying, maintaining, and running the car. Seifried (quoted in Whitelegg) coined the term "social speed" to give some idea of the average speed of different modes of transport once these hidden time costs are taken into account (Figure 2.1). Whitelegg writes:

> According to Seifried, the social speed of a typical bicycle is 14 kilometres per hour (kph), only three kph slower than that of a small car. If other external costs (air and noise pollution, accident costs, road construction costs and so on) are taken into account as well, then the small car is one kph slower than the bicycle (p.132).

Studies show that people have a travel time budget. Average journey-to-

Fig. 2.1 Average social speeds of the bicycle and the car

Average speed	15 km/h	40km/h	60km/h
Amount of time spent at work to earn yearly cost of the mode*	15 hrs	470 hrs	400hrs
Average 'social' speed	14km/h	17km/h	21km/h
External Costs per Km		15Pf/Km	30Pf/Km
Average social speed when taking into account external costs	14km/h	13km/h	18km/h

* Calculated from the following figures. Annual costs: bicycle 120DM; small car 4,700DM; large car 16,000DM. Monthly net income of vehicle owner: bicycle 1,600DM; small car 1,600DM; large car 6,400DM.

Walking is the natural recreation for a man [woman or child] who desires not to absolutely suppress his intellect, but to turn it to play for a season.

Leslie Stephen, cited in Bernard Rudofsky, *Streets for People*

The typical American male devotes more than 1,600 hours a year to his car. He sits in while it goes and while it stands idling. He parks it and searches for it. He earns the money to put down on it and to meet the monthly instalments. He works to pay for petrol, tolls, insurance, taxes and tickets. He spends four of his sixteen waking hours on the road or gathering his resources for it... The model American puts in 1,600 hours to get 7,500 miles: less than five miles per hour. In countries deprived of a transportation industry, people manage to do the same, walking wherever they want to go, and they allocate only three to eight per cent of their society's time budget to traffic instead of 28 per cent.

Ivan Illich, *Energy and Equity*

work times have remained around the 20–30 minute mark since the times when most people walked to work (Manning, p.42). This phenomenon has caused Whitelegg to refer to a "time illusion" which results in "a theft of time." For example, compare a car owner who spends 30 minutes per day driving 20 kilometres to work with a bicyclist who spends the same time covering seven and a half kilometres. Car owners will feel that they are travelling faster. But in reality, when all the time costs are factored in, they are spending 70 minutes to cover the distance while the cyclist is spending only 32 minutes.

But perhaps the greatest time cost that is not factored in (and one not included in the social speed examples above) is time lost through health impacts. Let me illustrate this with a personal story. At age 44 I went to my doctor for a health check to find that my blood pressure was unacceptably high. He went to his bookshelves and pulled out some research that showed that at my age, and with my level of blood pressure, I would lose 18 years off my life. He then informed me that all I needed to bring my blood pressure down was 20 minutes exercise each day — which could be as simple as a brisk walk. By walking to work I could save 18 years.

Three doctors in Australia recently released a report called *Pedalling Health*. It states:

> Technology has all but replaced adult human effort in the home and workplace. The journey to work or school which until quite recently involved a walk to public transport or a cycle ride is now mostly by motor vehicle and the walk to the local shop is now a drive to a shopping centre. The population has become sedentary and health agencies in Australia are now grappling with the illness burden arising from this rapid reduction in physical activity. The cost of treating the adverse consequences using drugs and surgery is threatening to overwhelm our health-care system unless major change occurs.
>
> One scenario is to increase heath-care funding for treatment of illness through additional taxation and another is to increase exercise in the community again...
>
> The physical activities that are most health promoting are moderate, habitual and not seasonal...
>
> The significance of physical inactivity is its prevalence amongst Australians: 27% are sedentary, at least 55% have insufficient exercise to have any appreciable benefit, and only 15-20% have enough exercise for optimal protection. The cost of cardiovascular disease in Australia was almost $4 billion in 1989-90. The proportion of this cost attributable to lack of exercise as an independent risk factor was $1.2-1.6 billion in that year.

The savings to the community just in health costs of more people walking or cycling to work, school, or the shops are estimated at about $66-$88 for every person in Australia — enough to buy every resident a new bike every two to three years.

I have always found keeping exercise routines for longer than about three months impossible. I don't even buy exercise machines because I know they will wind up collecting dust because I don't have the discipline. Apparently I am not alone. This phenomenon has caused major health authorities like Health Canada to shift their health promotion emphasis from trying to get people to exercise regularly to what they term "active transportation." In other words, use walking or cycling as a form of transportation. It is much easier to keep a routine of walking to work, school or the local shops than it is to get up half an hour earlier every morning, ride an exercise bike, and then sit in your car in congested traffic.

I tried it. For a number of years I walked 6 kilometres (4 miles) to work every day. I discovered it was not only good for my health, it became an invaluable time to relax and think. It fed my creative reservoir.

Instead of going to a gym, think of your walk to work, the shops, or school as paying yourself to get some exercise. You save on gym fees and transport costs. You also save the time you would have spent in the gym or riding an exercise bike to get fit. You may also give yourself a gift of 18 extra years of life. Now that makes spending a little extra time walking to work seem like a very wise investment! Think of walking or cycling somewhere as saving and creating extra time — not as costing you time.

The potential reductions available by replacing some trips with walking and cycling vary from city to city and from suburb to suburb. However, in the first Car Activity Diary exercise undertaken in Brisbane, respondents indicated that walking alone could reduce their car use by 5%. In fact, 47% of their car trips were shorter than 3 km, and 81% shorter than 6 km. That means that 81% of all trips were within walking or cycling distance. The trips that were shorter than 6 km constituted 48% of their total car use.

There is another mental shift that makes walking, cycling, or using public transport more attractive. This part of your day can become far more than just a time when you relax and reflect. It can become a very valuable social and cultural event. For example, it is an ideal opportunity for some people-watching.

Walking and cycling have social and cultural rewards — unexpected events that can enrich your day: birds feeding their young in a nest, a conversation with a stranger, even music.

Replacing some car trips with walking, cycling, or using public transport should be done not only because it's good for the environment or because it helps reduce traffic city-wide or because it saves you money. It improves your health — physically, emotionally, spiritually, socially, and culturally.

Reduction Strategy 2: Remove Unnecessary Trips

Combine two or more trips

People like myself who have gone from being a car owner to relying mainly on walking and cycling for transport find that a strange thing happens to our trip-making. We start organizing our trips more efficiently. One of the simplest ways of organizing your trips more efficiently is trip-chaining or trip-blending. This is where you save up your non-urgent trips and combine them into a single trip. A fridge organizer (a simple pad on the fridge) can help your household note non-urgent trips to combine them into a single trip.

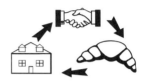

Trip-chaining can also be very effective in the workplace. Some people have found that by leaving their car at home one, two, or three days per week, they are forced to organize their work-related trips more efficiently.

Car pool and share rides

Another way of reducing the number of trips you make is to share a ride with someone else — what is referred to as car pooling. You can do this not just for work, but for kids' sport and other weekly activities that you may share with your neighbors.

Telecommute

Working from home one or more days per week — telecommuting — also reduces the number of work trips you have to make. Long-term, I am an advocate of building telecommute cottages in every neighborhood. It worries me that the trend for people to work from home via computer further weakens social contact and social networks. Telecommute cottages should combine the latest telecommunications and office machine facilities with other community facilities such as a coffee shop, child-care, library, or home-delivery depot. In this way, the telecommute cottage can become a centre for the revitalisation of neighborhood life. As I will show in the chapter on Street Reclaiming, in many parts of the world, streets are wide enough to establish these facilities right in the street as part of the reclaiming process.

Telephone, fax, and email

Some trips can be replaced by using the telephone, fax, or email. As the yellow pages advertisement says in Australia: "Let your fingers do the walking." As someone who relies on alternative means of transport, I have learnt very quickly the value of phoning around first to make sure a business has the product I require.

Home and office deliveries

Home and office deliveries are also a way to cut the number of trips we make. There are a whole range of innovations that are yet to take place in this arena. Because of the increase in the number of households in which all adults work outside the home, home deliveries have become much less viable. But there is no reason why a "home delivery depot" can not be established in neighborhoods — a place where home deliveries are dropped off and collected as people arrive home from work. This may be someone's house, the corner store, the telecommute cottage, or a storage area in the street itself.

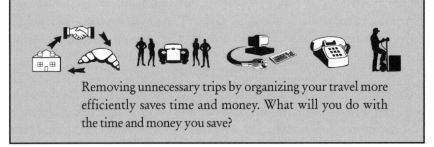

Removing unnecessary trips by organizing your travel more efficiently saves time and money. What will you do with the time and money you save?

Reduction Strategy 3: Reduce Trip Lengths

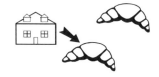

Shopping and employing locally

Shopping and employing locally helps reduce trip lengths. By thinking carefully, or checking the yellow pages of a telephone directory, you can often find the thing you want closer. And where possible, employ the tradespeople who live closest to your house.

However, shopping and employing locally does more than reduce trip lengths and therefore your car use. It helps create a stronger local economy and jobs market. This prosperity will eventually feed back into your pocket. Here's how it works. Imagine for a moment that for every $100 you earn, you are spending $80 on products and services and $20 on burning fuel to get access to these goods and services. If you reduce your fuel burning to $10, you now have $90 to spend on goods and services. Even if by shopping and employing locally you wind up spending $90 on the same goods and services, you are still ahead because you have saved time and a greater percentage of the money you spend will stay in the local economy helping to employ local people. Let me give a real-life example. A shoe merchant in Adelaide told me he once had six shoe stores in neighborhood shopping centres. He closed them down and invested in a mega-shoe store in a regional shopping centre. The total turnover from the one mega-store was roughly the same as the combined turnover from the six neighborhood stores. Although he had reduced his staffing requirements from 8 people to 2 people, his profit margin was still the same because the mega-store had higher capital costs — management required him to replace the carpet every two years whether it needed it or not and his rent had to cover the acres of carparking spaces needed for people to shop at his mega-store. What he hadn't counted on was that although his profits remained the same, he now had six fewer employees, which was six fewer people that could afford to buy shoes.

Reducing your trip lengths by shopping locally saves time and travel costs. Think of shopping locally or using local tradespeople as buying yourself or your kids a job.

Street space saved through reduced car use must be reused as exchange space — places of social, cultural, and economic exchange.

Reduction Strategy 4: Reuse Saved Space

These first three reduction strategies — replace, remove, reduce — are ones that your household can implement immediately. The next two reduction strategies are ones that your street, neighborhood, or entire city can implement.

As noted earlier, reducing car use saves valuable road and car parking spaces. This space must be reused because

- if the space is not reused, other people will simply expand their inefficient car use, resulting in a reshuffle of inefficiencies but not in their reduction
- reusing the saved space to make the alternative transport choices more attractive allows people to reduce their car use even further
- converting the saved movement space (roads and carparks) back into exchange space (shops, parks, houses, community facilities) creates a more efficient city with a great range of facilities "just around the corner." This enables further reductions in car use, which saves even more space which can be reused to improve choices, etc.

Street Reclaiming — reusing street space

The next chapter will deal in detail with how the space that is saved through traffic reduction can be reused to reclaim your street. However, it is important to underline the role that this reclaiming plays in the overall traffic reduction strategy. One of the reasons people do not walk or cycle for short trips is that the walking and cycling environment is both dangerous and often not very stimulating. If streets were transformed from linear movement corridors into a series of "outdoor living rooms," each stamped with the unique personality of local residents, then the journey on foot or cycle would become an adventure — a kind of place crawl. As you crossed the threshold from one room into the next, you would feel as if you were entering the intimate space of other people.

Ultimately, the restoration of the traditional role of the street for play, socializing, and cultural activities will also lessen the demand to travel to compensate for these lost activities. For example, the need to chauffeur children to organized sporting events or to their friend's house would lessen if children could reclaim their own streets for play. The need for senior citizens to drive to organized senior citizen clubs (where they basically interact with other senior citizens) would be lessened if senior citizens could sit in the street and talk with each other, the children who play there, and those who pass by. And instead of going to adult education classes, the rest of us could simply

Before there was any public transportation in London, something like fifty thousand people an hour used to pass over London Bridge on their way to work; a single artery. Railroad transportation can bring from forty to sixty thousand people per hour, along a single route, whereas our best expressways, using far more space, cannot move more than four to six thousand cars.

Mumford (1958), cited in Roberto Brambilla, *More Streets for People*

Motorized vehicles create new distances which they alone can shrink. They create them for all, but can only shrink them for a few.

Ivan Illich, cited in Rodney Tolley, *The Greening of Urban Transport*

sit with these senior citizens and absorb their collective wisdom while at the same time reconnecting ourselves to the creative genius resident in all children's play.

Reclaiming streets therefore provides a wide range of social and cultural activities right in our front yard for which we are currently forced to travel. And one could argue that the social and cultural activities that street reclaiming restores are of a superior quality to those for which we currently travel. As discussed in Chapter One, the planned social and cultural events (such as organized sporting events or the senior citizens club) are one-dimensional, lacking the diversity which is essential for creative life. In organized sporting events children play with children of the same age and same sex, and the rules of the game are set by adults. By contrast, play in the street requires them to incorporate a broader range of age-groups in the play. They must learn how to adapt the space for their play — creating their own field of play, thereby learning the skills of place-making. They are free to invent their own rules of the game — rules that are negotiated to accommodate all the needs of all the players. The game must also accommodate the needs of the other people using the same space: the car drivers, the adults talking on the street corner, the crabby man on the corner who doesn't like them walking on his grass, etc. Play in the street therefore teaches them a much broader range of social, spatial, and creative skills. Similarly, the interactions that the senior citizen has in the street are always potentially richer than those engaged in in a senior citizen club.

Street reclaiming can, however, restore more than just these lost social and cultural exchanges. As we shall see in the next chapter, it is possible to restore some of the lost economic exchanges. Many streets are wide enough to include facilities such as convenience stores, home-delivery depots, telecommute cottages, farmers' markets, etc. Again, this reduces the need for car movements by bringing the economic exchange and work opportunity closer to home.

Reallocating space to alternative transport modes

Alternative transport modes (walking, cycling, and using public transport) are much more space-efficient than the private car. In space efficiency terms, it makes a lot of sense to take existing space, which is used exclusively for car traffic, and to reallocate this to the alternative means. Again, this creates one of those virtuous cycles (Figure 2.2) where making the alternatives more attractive allows more people to reduce their car use, which allows for more space to be reallocated to the alternatives.

A classic story of space reallocation is the Curitiba bus system in Brazil. (see p.77.) Using dedicated busways and a host of innovations, they have created a "surface subway" which is four times more efficient than other city bus systems. However, I believe we have not yet even scratched the surface of how space saved through traffic reduction could be reallocated to highly efficient public transport systems (see *My Fantasy* below).

Creating facilities closer to home and work

Parking spaces, particularly in local shopping centres, could be reused to create a greater range of facilities closer to people's home and work, thus reducing the need to drive. The amount of space available for redevelopment is staggering. Hart and Spivak report in their book *Automobile Dependence and Denial:*

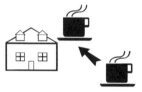

> Our observations in Los Angeles lead us to believe that, at present levels of service (convenience), each vehicle requires eight parking spaces — one full-use space at home, one at work, the remainder in fractional-use spaces at supermarkets, retail stores, doctors, dentists, restaurants and other business establishments throughout the city. (p.31)

Researchers in Brisbane concluded that cars consumed three times more space than the home of their owner.

In the next chapter we will also explore, how community facilities and even commercial facilities can be created in residential streets.

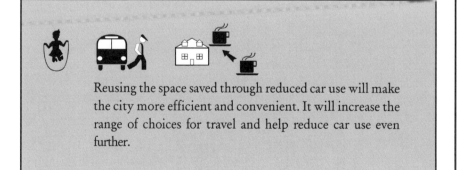

Reusing the space saved through reduced car use will make the city more efficient and convenient. It will increase the range of choices for travel and help reduce car use even further.

MY FANTASY

Instead of a car, people have a "lounge chair on wheels" which can be powered by peddling or a small rechargeable electric motor. At the centre of each neighborhood is a "pick up station" where these mobile lounge chairs can plug onto a "conveyor belt" — no waiting, no delay. You type your desired destination into a key-pad in the armrest and your mobile armchair is automatically connected into the right conveyor belts at transfer points. When you arrive at your destination, you self-power or use the small electric motor in your mobile arm chair to go the last part of the distance. By eliminating waiting delays, you can travel much slower on the journey but still get there faster.

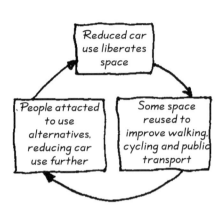

Fig. 2.2 How reusing space to improve transport choices helps reduce car use even further.

Above: Buxtehude has created "cycle arterials" where cars and bikes have traded places!

Below: In this Delf one-way street, cyclists are given half the street space and allowed to ride in both directions. But look which lane the lady with a child on the back is using. Half the street is not enough.

During the pre-industrial age, Barcelona and its environs — Grácia Sants — devoted approximately 17% of their land to their transport system... Since the car came onto the scene, the development of urban nuclei has been accompanied by a growing occupation of roadways and car parks. At the present time, any urban development plan devotes at least 40% of useful space to roads and car parks.

Salvador Rueda, *The Sustainable City*

The Curitiba Story

Driven by lack of resources, Curitiba has striven to build a bus system that competes in performance with underground rail, but is 500 times cheaper. In fact, the inspiration for developing their system — nicknamed the "surface subway" — was to try and take all the advantages of underground rail and to build them into a bus system.

The first advantage of rail is that it runs on its own exclusive line. So the first step for Curitiba was to develop exclusive busways right to the city centre. If a normal bus, running in normal traffic, can move X people per day, the exclusive ways doubled that to 2X. As patronage rose, the next innovation was the introduction of articulated buses — which increased the carrying capacity to 2.5X. Next came the quantum leap in thinking. What if they could load and unload passengers as they do in an underground system — fares prepaid and loading through multiple doorways which are at the same level as the bus? So Curitiba invented a simple glass and steel tube boarding station at which you pay your fare as you enter. When the bus pulls alongside, ramps fold down from the bus to connect with the tube station allowing a level transfer between the bus and the station. Those in wheelchairs, or those with mobility restrictions can then take as much time as they need to negotiate the stairs at the end of the station or use the hydraulic lift. Meanwhile, the bus is speeding to its next station. By adding extra doors to the bus, the tube stations raised the carrying capacity to 3.2X. But the system was still strained, so they invented the bi-articulated bus — a bus that carries up to 270 people. With this, the carrying capacity rose to 4X.

Twenty transfer stations are now located around the city. Local feeder buses collect people from their neighborhoods and drop them at the transfer stations. From there you can catch an inner or outer circumferential service connecting the transfer stations. Or you can catch a "speedy bus" which uses the exclusive lanes. You can travel anywhere in the city for a flat fare of 40 US cents — called a "social fare" as the poorer people live on the city outskirts. What is amazing is that the system is not subsidized and is run by an interesting mix of public and private enterprise. The city determines what services there should be and provides the infrastructure such as the tube stations and exclusive lanes. Private companies provide the buses, drivers, and fare collectors. They get paid per kilometre of bus service, not per passenger. The entire system is run from the farebox. Since 1991, when the Speed Buses were introduced, 28% of all new riders are people who once drove. 75% of commuters ride the buses. In 1974, when the system was first started, it served 27,000 passengers per day. In 1994, it was serving over 800,000 passengers per day. Even though Curitiba has the second highest rate of car ownership in Brazil (one car for every three people), its gasoline use per head of population is 30% below that of eight comparable Brazilian cities.

The Walking School Bus gets kids to school safely while giving them exercise and building a stronger sense of community.

Reduction Strategy 5: Reciprocate for Mutual Benefit

Because traffic is a *collective* problem, perhaps the most promising reduction strategies are *collective* solutions.

Walking School Bus

The Walking Bus is an invention to overcome the problems of traffic safety and perceptions of stranger danger. A "Walking Bus Driver" walks a set route each morning and afternoon and picks up children at Walking Bus Stops. While I first proposed the idea of the Walking Bus in *Reclaiming Our Cities and Towns (Towards an Eco-City)* in 1992, it is only now starting to be implemented in some cities — most notably in Canada where Health Canada has put money into a national Walking School Bus program. I think there are some difficulties with trying to organize Walking Buses at the entire school level. Ultimately, I believe they will be best organized from the neighborhood level. Organizing them from the school level involves a process of mapping safe routes, finding bus drivers, back-up drivers, etc. This is not to say that this approach should not continue but rather that the level of organization and coordination would be much less if the Walking Bus was implemented as part of neighborhood strategies to reduce car use. Later I will describe how streets can implement their own traffic reduction program using a street party. I can imagine someone at the street party saying "Well, lets start a Walking Bus." Mrs Jones, who is retired, says: "I would love to be the driver. It would force me to get that exercise I need and it would be lovely to interact with the kids." Mr Smith responds: "Well, Betty, I will join you as your back-up driver. If you get sick or want to go on holidays, I'll be there to fill in." George who is a handyperson says: "I've got some wheels and stuff in the garage which I can knock up into the bus." And on the spot the safest route is mapped. And it all starts the following Monday.

For the Walking Bus to be a success, it needs the following features:

- One or more drivers. These need not be parents. They can be retired people, grandparents, or people who work from home.
- Designated back up drivers.
- The safest route mapped and designated pick-up points.
- High visibility. If a trolley of some kind is used as a bus, it should be brightly coloured and have safety flags high enough to be seen above cars. The driver can wear a safety vest which is available from road-safety equipment shops. I also suggest that an adult or the oldest child be a "conductor" at the rear of the bus to keep the group together. They too can wear a safety vest which for fun can have tail-lights painted on the back and even a number plate. Children can all be issued a brightly coloured hat which identifies them as part of the Walking Bus and increases visibility.
- A "bus" in which children can place their bags and in which rain or snow gear can be kept. After much experimentation, I have found that a design based on a 3-wheel baby jogger works best (see opposite page.) For increased safety, the bus should be pushed rather than pulled so that it enters the roadway before the driver or children enter the roadway.

Expand the Walking Bus by inviting others in the neighborhood to join in as a way of getting regular exercise and as a social outing.

Bike Maintenance Clinics

On a regular basis, your street may organize a bike maintenance clinic which could be combined with a sidewalk barbecue or some other social event. People would bring their bikes and help each other perform regular maintenance. There could even be a street tool kit and spare parts supply, paid for by a small contribution from each household.

Car Sharing Clubs

In 1996, Car Sharing Clubs were operating in over 250 European cities and had over 20,000 members. The basic idea behind the clubs is that instead of owning your own car, you are part of a club that owns a fleet of cars. These clubs are located in your neighborhood within easy walking distance of your home. You pay a small joining fee to cover basic administration costs. When you need to use a car, you book the car of your choice through a central booking agency run by the club itself or by a taxi or bus company. At the end of the month, you get a bill for your car use depending on what size vehicle you drove, the distance, and the length of time and time of day you had the car.

The advantages for club members are significant. There is no need to outlay capital to buy a vehicle. Provided you keep your car use to a minimum, this saves significant money. In other words, instead of paying the full capital costs of a vehicle, you may only be paying the capital costs of a quarter of a vehicle or a tenth of a vehicle. Participants also have greater flexibility in the vehicles they can use. If they need to move furniture, they have access to a pick-up truck. If they need to take their kid and friends to a beach party, they have access to a van. If they want to visit friends on a farm, they have access to a compact car. If they want to impress the girlfriend, they have access to a sports car. The club also offers significant time savings by looking after all maintenance of the vehicles — no more washing cars or booking them in for a service, etc.

The clubs also offer a significant incentive to use cars more efficiently. Because the real costs of your car use are much more transparent (you know exactly how much it is costing you to drive each kilometre/mile), and because you have to book the vehicle, you organize your travel much more efficiently. In Europe, participants typically find that their car use drops by half.

Car sharing clubs in Europe are now offering a total "mobility service" which they negotiate with transit authorities and taxi companies. For example, in Bremen (Germany) you can buy a transit pass that has a smart-card inside which is your key to the Car Share Club vehicles. The outer "case" is a monthly or yearly transit ticket. The rationale is that you can have total flexibility —

public transport or private car — all in one package. In fact, some transit authorities are now setting up Car Sharing Clubs at transit stops and promoting "total mobility packages."

Shop-and-Employ-Locally Incentive Programs

Later I will describe the concept of *Traffic Reduction Treaty Streets* — streets that implement a traffic reduction plan in exchange for a broad range of benefits. The economic benefits for these streets need not be just the immediate savings they get from reduced car use. They could use their buying power to convince local merchants to offer discounts to people who belong to *Traffic Reduction Treaty Streets*.

One such scheme that I have devised is called the *SmartMove Rewards Card*. Merchants would offer a discount to card-holder based on how customers arrive at the store. For example, they may offer a 5% discount if you arrive by car, but a 10% discount if you don't use a car to get there. The rationale is quite simple. By them encouraging a reduction in car use and local shopping, there will be more money circulating in the local economy. That means greater profits and job opportunities for everyone. In addition, less congestion on the roads makes all businesses more profitable. Store owners may also band together to find ways of cooperatively offering a home delivery service.

Businesses may become the provocateurs in encouraging streets to become *Traffic Reduction Treaty Streets*. In fact, they could even mastermind innovations like a promenade loop which connects major activity centres in a neighborhood: shops, school, library, park, and transit stop. One sidewalk on one side of the road is enhanced to concentrate pedestrian traffic. The loop is made attractive with seating, sculptures, drinking fountains, exercise areas, etc. The local merchants may encourage all the streets on such a loop to become *Traffic Reduction Treaty Streets* and to participate in the design and building of the loop. They may put some resources into enhancing the loop where it passes through the local shopping centre.

Universal transit pass

Universities in Boulder, Colorado, and Seattle, Washington have developed a universal transit pass. They approached the transit authority to find out how much their students contributed to the farebox. They then struck a deal with the transit authority to give them this amount up front at the start of the year. Next they apportioned this cost across the entire student body and gave every student a transit card. In the case of Seattle, some of the cost of the transit cards was covered by raising car parking charges. The result is that students get a universal transit card for a ridiculously small amount

A promenade loop can connect facilities in the neighborhood.

In 1939 the Los Angeles Railway Corporation paid taxes of $950, 741 and still made an operating profit of $760,411 ... In total, about $175 million was paid to government bodies by Chicago transit companies from 1907 to 1931.

David J St Clair, *The Motorization of American Cities*

of money. In fact, Boulder transport people told me that if they tried to take the cards away, there would be riots on campus. Boulder is trying to extend this scheme to large employers.

But I wonder why the scheme cannot be applied to a whole city, making public transport virtually free. A range of means could be used to raise the equivalent of what is currently collected in fares. For example, a small charge could be placed on all rateable properties, with commercial properties carrying a slightly higher charge on the grounds that reduced car use is good for business. This could be supplemented with a small levy on all non-residential carparking spaces, the rationale being that every carparking space must be serviced by roads to get the cars to the parking lot and that this imposes significant costs on government (including infrastructure costs associated with urban sprawl caused by the heavy space demands of private cars).

The abolition of fares and the creation of a universal transit pass have a number of other significant advantages. Because tickets do not have to be checked, boarding can be through multiple doors, speeding up the loading and unloading process. If platforms or raised curbs were created at the bus stops and fold-out ramps connected the bus to these platforms, loading could also be at level, allowing people with mobility difficulties easy access. This would speed the entire system up by as much as 25%. This increase in productivity can be recycled as a gain in service level (to augment the increased demand for services) or in decreased operating costs.

For those who argue that car drivers should not be forced to contribute to a public transport system they do not use, there are a range of very powerful counter arguments (see next page.)

Schemes that reciprocate for mutual benefit provide win-win solutions. By working together, we can invent structures and financial arrangements that deliver collective benefits from which individuals can draw off more than their original investment.

The case for free public transport

Too much traffic on the roads delays everyone and is currently costing every driver significant time and money. If drivers invest a small amount in the public transport system, they actually save themselves time and money (they are paying others to stop costing them money!). There is also a rational and moral argument that says that cities are essentially a cooperative enterprise. The unspoken agreement is that the citizens agree to share a common space in order to maximize both their individual and collective good. Part of that common property shared by all citizens is the streets — a place for social, cultural and economic exchanges and a place where people can move to reach social, cultural, and economic exchanges. The most efficient means of moving through this public domain is walking, cycling, or using collective forms of transport. If some members of the collective enterprise decide that they would prefer to use a more private means of transport, they have a moral obligation to ensure that the viability of the collective enterprise is not undermined or damaged by this decision. If it is, then they have a moral obligation to pay for the repair of whatever damage their decision inflicts on the collective enterprise. In plain English, this means that car drivers should pay the equivalent of a public transport fare for every trip they make in their car so that the publicly provided means of transport can be maintained at the same level it would be operating at if they were using it. Why should the rest of the citizens bear a downgraded public transport service because car drivers choose to use a private means of transport rather than that constructed by the collective enterprise?

If we view the city as a collective enterprise and public transport (which incidentally includes walking and cycling) as the means of movement provided by the collective enterprise, then it makes no sense at all to be collecting fares one at time. For a start, collecting these small sums of money is incredibly inefficient. (Authorities often ignore the costs of collecting the fare, including the vehicle downtime created by the delay of collecting the fare.) It makes much more sense, both from an efficiency point of view and from a social justice point of view, to find mechanisms of collection that spread the costs evenly across all members of the collective enterprise and makes sure that those who do damage to the system (as private car users do) pay for adequate repair and maintenance of the system.

There is an economic rationalist argument that says that free public transport will lead to distortions in the market, with people abusing the system and using it more than they need too. There is validity in this argument. But this is exactly the situation we have with roads at the moment. Society (through taxes which everyone pays regardless of whether they own a car or not) provides the infrastructure free of charge to motorists. There is no doubt that this has led to gross distortions in the market. However, there is one important difference. Free public transport would be a public service that is open to all — children, the aged, those with disabilities, the poor. Free public roads are a service available only to those who have a driver's licence and enough wealth to buy a car. There are many services we provide in a city free of charge because the city is by nature a collective enterprise. We do not charge people to walk on sidewalks which are provided at public expense. An important principle within the collective enterprise is that the entire society should provide only those services which are democratically available to all.

The overuse of free public transport is likely to be far less than the overuse of free public roads by motorists because the use of public transport requires a walk at either end of the trip. The experience of the Car Share Clubs in Europe suggests that this in itself is an incentive to organize travel more efficiently.

In Summary

By using the first three traffic reduction strategies, households can immediately reduce their car use substantially — generally by 25–50%. These reduction strategies include replacing some trips with walking, cycling, or using public transport; removing unnecessary trips by saving up non-urgent trips and combining them into a single trip; using car pooling, telecommuting, and home and office deliveries; and reducing trip lengths by shopping and employing locally.

The next two reduction strategies are ones that can be employed by a street,  neighborhood, group of neighborhoods, or the entire city. They provide longer-term savings that build on the savings achieved by individual households. Space that is saved through reduced car use should be reused for street reclaiming, reallocation of space to other transport modes, and the creation of facilities closer to home and work. Perhaps the most promising strategy for reducing traffic involves reciprocating for mutual benefit, in other words schemes like Walking School Buses and bike maintenance clinics, car sharing clubs, shop-and-employ-locally incentive schemes, and universal transit passes.

We are still at the infancy stages of the traffic reduction revolution. The examples given in this chapter are just the starting point of what will eventually become a multi-billion dollar industry. Just as the waste reduction revolution required recycling bins at every household before it became part of mainstream cultural practice, the traffic reduction revolution will require the widespread introduction of hardware innovations such as Walking School Buses, Car Sharing Clubs, and SmartMove Rewards Cards. But out there in the creative marshlands of people's minds are probably a thousand other traffic reduction innovations — just waiting to be invented.

chapter three

STREET RECLAIMING
Design Guidelines

Chalk is a great medium for psychological reclaiming. Create temporary murals — or get the adults playing hop-scotch.

Shelling peas on the sidewalk is an act of psychological reclaiming. All you need is a seat on the sidewalk — and some peas.

Reclaiming the Traditional Roles of the Street

As noted earlier, historically streets were not just used for movement. They were the epicenter of community life, a place for socializing, children's play, drama, education, celebrations, social events, and economic activity. These important social, cultural, and economic functions have been slowly eroded as car traffic has exerted its dominance. *Street Reclaiming* means winning back your street as the social and cultural epicentre of your neighborhood life.

The next chapter suggests a practical program for your street to work together in implementing a *Traffic Reduction Plan* and *Street Reclaiming*. Although it may seem like putting the cart before the horse to discuss street reclaiming before discussing this program, my goal is to get you so excited about the possibilities of reclaiming your street that you will be highly motivated to do the necessary ground work. The ideas in this book are built on incentive and celebration. None of us minds the task of baking a cake — if we get some of the enjoyment of eating it. This chapter is a picture of street reclaiming that will hopefully get your taste buds salivating.

Street reclaiming has two distinctive components: psychological reclaiming and physical reclaiming. Psychological reclaiming reinstates the lost social, cultural, and economic functions of the street. This can be done without taking one square inch of roadway away from cars. Physical reclaiming takes back some of the physical roadspace and converts this to exchange space.

However, I must sound one note of caution. As a result of reading this book or undertaking the activities in the next chapter, the people in your street may well see your street through new eyes. But the motorists who use your street may still see your street as "their" road. The changes you make to your street must be seen in the larger context of helping to seed a city-wide cultural change in attitudes to streets. You may therefore need to exert some patience in explaining to motorists that they must share the street with other users. The changes you make to your street are an important part of this educational process. Later I will suggest that you should not use elements whose primary focus is to "punish" motorists. Rather, you should provide an environment which makes motorists want to slow down to absorb the ambience.

In this chapter you will find boxes with light bulbs on top. These are ideas boxes. Some ideas are practical. Some are "off the wall." They are included to stimulate your creativity. Be adventurous.

The street, in fact, is the most important thread in a city's fabric. It knits the city together as a city. To kiss the street goodbye is the kiss of death for a city.

Roberta Brandes Gratz, *The Living City*

EVER-CHANGING PSYCHOLOGICAL RECLAIMING

Ever-changing streets are the most interesting. Try these activities:

- Have children create posters that you display on the side of the road.
- Leave up the balloons and streamers from your street party and continue the festive spirit.
- Create large chalk murals on the road.
- Place old lounge chairs on a street corner or in a carparking space.
- Use rubbish or recycling bins as props for sidewalk art.
- Decorate parked cars — use them to display banners and art pieces.
- Turn car trailers into a temporary carpark garden and move it each day.

Taking a seat out onto the sidewalk or placing a lounge chair in a parking bay is the easiest form of psychological reclaiming.

Psychological reclaiming

Earlier I cited the research of Donald Appleyard that shows that cars have an ever-increasing zone of influence as the volume and speed of traffic increases. Historically, we have given up our home territory as traffic has exerted this growing influence. Psychological reclaiming is to reverse this trend and be assertive about our rights to the traditional uses of the street. Psychological reclaiming therefore starts by seeing your street through new eyes — not as the sole domain of traffic but as your "outdoor living room."

Psychological reclaiming through activities

Psychological reclaiming means being proactive and not waiting for the traffic on your street to shrink. Car culture will change when people simply take the street back and start using their street for children's play, socializing, and community building. Experience says that traffic slows down when drivers perceive that a street is no longer their sole domain and that traveling through it has become riskier because of increased pedestrian or resident activity. The first step in reclaiming your street is to take the initiative and simply to start using the street as your living room.

For example, you can take a chair out onto the sidewalk and supervise your children playing on the sidewalk or road. If you don't have children to supervise, read a book or shell peas. Invite your neighbors to bring a chair out and form a conversation circle on the sidewalk. If you want to be a little more assertive, place your chairs in a carparking space on the side of the street. If you want to be even more assertive, edge them out into the roadway and narrow the traffic lane.

Walking your children to school or cycling are also forms of psychological reclaiming. As you walk or cycle, see the street as belonging more to you than to the motorists. As a street community or neighborhood, you may organize regular events like having a monthly barbecue on the sidewalk or in some carparking spaces.

Psychological reclaiming through physical changes

There is a wide range of physical changes you can make to your street to alter the psychological feel of your street without necessarily taking away any road space. These include:

- Seating and other sidewalk facilities. These encourage people to use the street more but also send a clear message to motorists that this is not just a traffic corridor.
- Sidewalk banners and sculptures. Hanging banners on the edge of the sidewalk visually narrows a road which encourages drivers to go slower. The design of the

We need the art of relationship, weaving the elements of buildings, trees, levels, nature, water, traffic into spaces for people so they become identifiable places .... Towns are about carnivals and street theatre, celebrations and marches, about festivals, saints days and Christmas parades, rugby internationals and public protests; jazz band festivals at Brecon and miners' gala days in Cardiff, and the opening of parliament, and Rememberace Day. Cities are about proud tree-lined avenues and promenades, and sea front boulevards, and fine vistas of spires and towers. Design entails creating the form and atmosphere in which the recurring drama of public life takes place.

Graham King, *"No particular place"*

banners can also be used to send a message to drivers. Designs which include children playing, local wildlife and fauna, or other things that are valued and celebrated by the neighborhood give a signature to your street much as the art pieces in someone's house stamp the house as belonging uniquely to them. Similarly, sculptures can send very powerful messages that a street is not just for cars. The sculpture may be as simple as a kid's tricycle painted in bright colours and mounted on a post; a cricket bat, pine box, and cricket ball; a hockey stick; or car parts used as a planter.

- Overhead banners and sculptures. These visually enclose your street giving it the more intimate feel of a room. This hemming in of the street space will cause traffic to slow down. However, the design of these overhead pieces is also important in giving your street a signature and conveying messages about how the residents see the street.
- Road murals. They can be used to visually break up a street into smaller "rooms." The driver gets the feeling that they are passing over thresholds into yet another private space. They must also drive over someone's valued art piece. Be sure to use non-slip paint specially formulated for roads.

The next section on physical reclaiming contains many design ideas that you can include in this phase of your reclaiming. For example, you can develop a theme or use any of the devices that do not physically take road space away from the cars.

An immediate start

Psychological reclaiming in your street is something that can start immediately. Organizing a street party is discussed in the next chapter. You may need to clear some of the physical changes such as banners with your council but there are plenty of things, some of them temporary, which you can do right now (see feature box previous page). Be innovative.

It is essential that people do not get bogged down in believing that nothing good can happen in their street unless they physically take some of the roadbed away from cars. Taking it away psychologically is far more important. That is why the initial emphasis should be on ways of psychologically reclaiming the street.

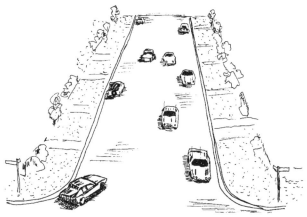

Before and after: psychological reclaiming which does not take physical space away from the car but takes it over psychologically by breaking the street into "rooms."

You can literally create a living room in your street — complete with floor rug, lounge chairs, and a TV (screen taken out and used as a community notice board).

Rocks in Boulder mall: simple, unpretentious play equipment that leave room for kids to use their imagination.

Physical Reclaiming

Taking back part of the road space

Physical reclaiming means taking some of the road space currently used by cars and converting it into spaces that will enhance the social, cultural, and economic life of your neighborhood. This process is very different to traditional traffic calming, whose sole aim is to provide a disincentive to motorists speeding. Again I wish to emphasise that psychological reclaiming of your street should happen before moving on to physical reclaiming.

I do not believe that any neighborhood has the right to reclaim its streets while contributing to the destruction of someone else's. There is therefore a moral obligation on those wishing to reclaim their street that they first ensure that they have reduced their own car use to a minimum and that when driving, they act like guests in someone else's living room.

Themes

A theme can tie your entire design together. In the overall design process, you may actually start with a theme. Or the theme may emerge as you do the detailed design. Here are some ideas for themes:

Play themes: Be careful not to over-design play spaces. Children need to develop the skills of taking raw space, converting it into their own space, and then re-inventing the entire space an hour later. For example, one of the most popular pieces of play equipment I have ever seen in a public street were three large rocks in the Boulder, Colorado, mall. Kids could climb on them, turn them into space ships in a dark sky or pirate ships on a stormy sea. They were like pieces of play dough that could be endlessly re-fashioned. Much modern play, like organized sport, removes this spontaneity and flexibility, killing off diversity and creativity. The design should include "secret spaces," places where children feel that they can hide from the adult world and invent their own reality. This may be as simple as an enclosed space for parking a car, which, when not being used for this purpose, provides a blank secret space.

The theme of play street should set a tone rather than be over-prescriptive.

Historical themes: Your street can celebrate the history of your neighborhood, some famous person who lived in your street, or some important event. If your street was once a market garden, you may establish a market garden theme. If trams once

PET ZOO

Imagine the surprise on the face of the motorists who rat-run down your street if one morning they found a pet zoo in the middle of your street.

rumbled down the centre of your street, you may put a tram in the middle of the road and convert it into a coffee shop, telecommute cottage, play area for children, or art shop. You can put up commemorative plaques or develop a totem pole that tells the story of your street.

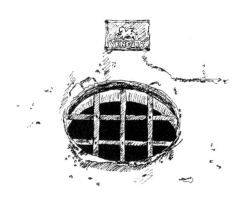

Fantasy themes: You may centre your design on a fairy tale or famous children's story. Or it may be designed around the theme of "imagine a world without cars." All the items in your street could be created from wrecked cars. The seating could be car seats, tree surrounds made from tires, the top cut from cars, and trees planted inside; a car could be used as a community notice board, kids could be given liberty to paint murals on some old cars, etc.

Art themes: Your street could become the world's longest outdoor art gallery. You could hold a regular artisans' market in your street. You could feature kids' art that changes on a weekly basis. You could hold outdoor art classes. You could have a permanent supply of chalk in roadside boxes and encourage street art.

Festive themes: Your street could become a circus with sculptured (or real) clowns crossing your street on high-wires (trapeze artists blown in the wind) or clowns peeking out from behind telephone poles. You may celebrate the four seasons with your street changing character at the change of the seasons. Your street could become a "stages-of-life paradise"' — a congratulations board registering all the special occasions for residents: birthdays, anniversaries, major achievements, etc. A special "celebration seat" could be placed outside the homes of those celebrating some event and people could be invited to come and interact with that person on their special day.

Changing themes: Your theme does not need to be set in stone forever. You may change your theme on the anniversary of signing the *Traffic Reduction Treaty* as a means of re-focusing the street on its commitment.

Gaudi's work in Barcelona has a strong fantasy theme which encourages a sense of fun and adventure.

Your Street as a Room

The genius of the older cities was that the notion of streets as both movement corridors and outdoor living rooms was built into the very design of the streets. As noted in Chapter One, the psychological message of "corridors" is that they are a place for movement. The psychological message of rooms is that they are an invitation to pause and engage in some kind of interaction. The streets that are most like rooms (for example, having an avenue of trees that provide strong "walls" and a "ceiling") are the most desirable addresses in a city.

In the modern city, where we have allowed the movement function to dominate over the exchange function, our streets have been designed as movement corridors and have lost their function as outdoor living rooms. If we are to reclaim our streets as places of social and cultural interaction, they need to be retrofitted in a way that emphasizes their role as outdoor rooms.

In the next chapter I suggest that streets should be reclaimed one block at a time. This runs counter to traditional traffic calming practices that work on entire neighborhood precincts. One of my reasons for arguing it should be done one street block at a time is that each block should be viewed as a single room in a network of rooms. If it is a long street block, it can even be divided into a number of smaller sub-rooms.

When you examine the street spaces that work best as outdoor rooms, you find that exactly the same design elements that make a room work indoors make it work outdoors. What follows is an exploration of those design elements.

The "campos" in Venice are a prime example of "outdoor rooms" connected by passageways. Most campos have a central feature such as a well which was once the social meeting point. We need to find equivalent meeting places in the modern city street — a community garden, outdoor coffee shop, or outdoor meeting area.

Portland paving has blocks with poems and witty sayings engraved.

Floors and pavements are the touchstones of a civilisation.

Bernard Rudofsky, *Streets for People*

NATIONAL STREET-HOCKEY COMPETITION

Street hockey is banned in many cities. Recently, one Canadian city said it would fine children playing street hockey. A national hockey star offered to pay the fine of any kids prosecuted. This gave me an idea. A neighborhood could host a National Street Hockey Competition, or a National Street Cricket Competition, or a National Street Games Competition. Let's do something significant to legitimize kids playing in the street. It could be the quickest way to reclaim our streets nationally.

Floors

Floors are the foundations upon which a room rests. In ancient cultures, floors and streets were considered sacred and making them beautiful was a sacred duty. Whether made of stone, clay bricks, timber, or rammed earth, they provided a sensual experience — the point of contact between the human body and mother earth.

In a street, the floor design can serve a multitude of purposes:

- Changes in texture or floor covering can signal your entry into a new space.
- Using borders is a classic way of defining the room (see drawing on page 91).
- A "rug" can create a room within the room.
- Patterns in the paving can give rhythm to a journey.
- Patterns can take large impersonal spaces and break them down into more human-scale spaces (see drawing opposite). These designs also give a sense of activity to the space.
- Paving design can be a work of art.

Freiburg streets feature flowing water channels and intricate paving.

- Paving design can be used for play.
- Special paving designs (like the rainbow serpent and dragon design below) can become "milestones" on a journey, breaking the journey into manageable segments.
- Paving design can inform — for example, give details of the history of a building or the local community.
- Paving design can amuse — like the witty phrases and lines from poems etched in Portland's sidewalks.

Think what you can do to make the floor in your outdoor living room a sensual, educational, fun experience. Your work could include

- street murals
- games boards
- paved paths
- ceramic rugs
- dry creek beds
- grass
- bridges over water
- gravel
- stepping stones.

BRING BACK THE GRASS

Cars only need two narrow tracks. Everything else can be grass. Do away with the sidewalks and let the whole street grow green.

This paving design in a Melbourne mall depicts the Aboriginal rainbow serpent and the Chinese dragon, symbolizing the multicultural background of local residents.

These two spaces are the same size. Paving design can break up large impersonal spaces into more human bite-sized pieces and impart a sense of "activity" in the space.

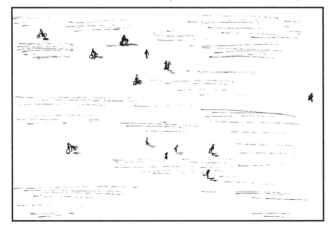

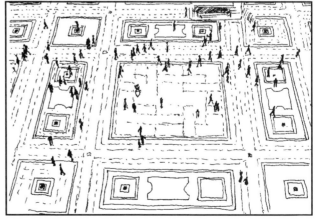

Walls are a blank canvas for art.

Walls

The intimacy of a room is created by defining the space with walls and strong boundaries. In older cities, the buildings came right to the street edge, thus providing a strong boundary for the outdoor room. In many Australian, North American, and British cities, houses are set well back from the street which does not help in creating this sense of the street as a room. You can strengthen the sense of enclosure by using landscaping, banners, or structures on the sidewalk or roadside to visually narrow the road and hem the space in.

Walls in the traditional street were also used as a canvas for art. Stone carvings were placed above doorways, in small recesses in walls, or on pedestals at the corner of buildings.

Before and after: Landscaping and banners are used to create "walls" that enclose the street, turning it into a more intimate room.

Doors and Windows

While walls create a sense of enclosure, blank walls are inherently boring and claustrophobic. Doors and windows create a sense of wonder and excitement and add to the drama of a room and public space. From the outside, they offer a glimpse into someone's private world. Even a drawn curtain evokes a sense of mystery. From the inside, doors and windows create a viewing frame into other worlds. This gives a balance between the intimacy of the room and the exposure to the excitement of worlds that lay beyond. It is important that your outdoor room maintain this balance by creating "viewing frames" into the more private spaces such as seating areas or people's front gardens. This selective transparency of the walls can be improved by having porches and verandahs that address and overlook the street and by not fencing off properties with solid walls and gates.

Contrast, variety, detail, surprise, drama, nooks, compactness, mixture of functions, nothing static, nothing boring — these are some of the things that make up a lively, well-functioning street.

Roberta Brandes Gratz , *The Living City*

Windows and doorways are an integral part of the street drama. They offer a glimpse into another world, and in so doing, stir our curiosity. And like people-watching, they provoke the storyteller in our head.

WINDOW SHOPPING

One of the great joys for me as a child was going window shopping. Imagine your street with coloured lights strung across the road and fairy lights in the trees. Lining the sidewalk are large , brightly lit boxes fitted with old recycled windows, each displaying artisans' work, local merchants' goods, or exotic products from around the world. Why not host an International Window Shopping Festival?

The gates need never close ....

A town or a village is a collective statement, within which individuals (families, homes) have their own identity. The art of living and building lies in harmonizing the fertile relationships between "my" house and "our" street, "my" street and "our" neighborhood, and "my" neighborhood and "our" town.

Jan Tanghe et al., *Living Cities*

Entryways

Grand rooms have a grand entryway. Entryways state that you are crossing from one type of space into another. This involves passing through a narrowed space that is framed in some special way. If one examines streets in Europe one finds a wide range of entryways: symbolic gateways, archways, or sophisticated structures that housed a gatekeeper in days bygone. Historically, some of these entryways were literally gates in a wall that could be closed to keep unwelcome guests out of a city quarter. They still offer the same message: as you cross the threshold, you are entering someone else's territory and you must act as a guest in that space. Unfortunately, "gated communities" have perverted this design principle by using the entryway as a means of exclusion rather than welcome.

I believe that entryway treatments may be one of the powerful tools in retrofitting streets in the Australian, North American, and British context to recapture this sense of streets as outdoor rooms which belong primarily to the local residents but which others can use as guests. Entryways need to be more substantial than the existing threshold treatments used in traffic calming schemes. They need not impede overall traffic flows and can even be used on major highways as the example from Curitiba in Brazil (see below) shows. Alternatively, they can be used as a device to restrict traffic. There is no reason why they cannot contain loft-type quarters which can be rented out or given to a "gatekeeper" who would perform certain public tasks for the street. It could be specially fitted as an artist's loft and the street could adopt their own artist. Rooms at ground level may be used as a home delivery depot or a small convenience store or coffee shop.

Imagine your street with an entry like this, housing your own street concierge!

ANY road can have a spectacular entry.
Left, highway in Curitiba, Brazil.
Right, major arterial in Melbourne, Australia.

Lights can create a ceiling.

Banners or washing — they both create a ceiling and movement.

Ceilings

The feeling of enclosure and intimacy in a room is enhanced by a ceiling. You can create a transparent ceiling in a street with banners, overhead sculptures, lanterns, lights, or flags. If you are prepared to wait 20 years, you can use trees to create an overhead canopy. If you have trees arching across the road, you can enhance this partial ceiling by hanging art pieces or objects from the branches. Mobiles that move in the wind can make your ceiling more interesting.

Lighting is sparkle, glow, jewellery, luminosity, magic, ambience, mystery, and much more.

David Kenneth Specter, *Urban Spaces*

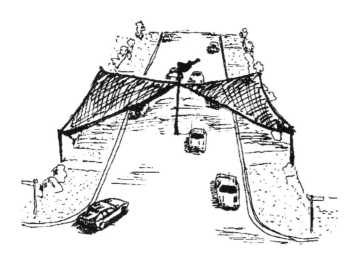

For instance, it simply never occurs to us to make streets into an oasis rather than deserts. In countries where their function has not yet deteriorated into highways and parking lots, a number of arrangements make streets fit for humans; pergola and awnings (that is awnings spread across a street), tent-like structures, or permanent roofs. All are characteristic of the Orient, or countries with an oriental heritage, like Spain.

Bernard Rudofsky, *Architecture without Architects*

Nooks and crannies

Rooms have bay windows, little intimate corners, spaces for solitude and reflection or private conversation. These are the "secret places" for both children and adults. An example of creating a secret space for children is the protected parking bay (see below). Loose chairs also enable people to create their own intimate spaces.

This protected parking space can also be used by children as a "secret space."

Furniture

Furniture in a room can serve multiple functions. It has the immediate function for which it is designed (chairs are used to sit on); it can serve an aesthetic function (the chair can be sensual or provocative, or tell a story); it can serve a social function (a particular arrangement of the chairs will encourage conversation, people-watching, or solitary reflection); and the placement of the furniture can help define a space and be used to help direct traffic flow in the room (the chair can help define a path through the room).

All these functions should be kept in mind when designing seating, tables, drinking fountains, or any other furniture items for your outdoor room.

BUS STOP FOCUS

If you have a bus stop in your street, make this the initial focus of your street reclaiming. Put out some armchairs for those waiting. Give them something interesting to do. A magazine stand. The morning paper. A mirror so they can finish dressing and do the make-up. A graffiti board with crayons. A community notice board.

Seating can be simple — or a work of art.

The richness and meaning of a place derives not from single items but from details which, taken together, contribute to a mosaic greater than the sum of its parts.

Peter Randall Page, in Patrick Nuttgens *The Furnished Landscape*

Loose chairs in Paris. Even empty chairs tell a story about those who last sat in them.

In Praise of Loose Chairs

Chairs that are movable and not bolted to the ground are an essential ingredient of any room. They allow people to instantly design a space for the particular needs of that moment. Two lovers may link the arms of their chairs. If there are three mutual friends, they will arrange the chairs in a triangle. If people wish to sit and reflect, they will move the chair away from where others are seated. If they want to people-watch, they can turn the chair to the pedestrian flow. If they don't, they can turn it away. They can choose to sit in the sun or the shade. They can improvise and use one chair as a table for bread and wine, a card table, or as a footstool to rest sore legs. Children will use them as battle ships, rockets going to the moon, or racing cars.

There is something internally liberating every time we are faced with a chair that is not nailed down. We are transformed from an anonymous resident into an urban designer deciding how that space will look for one moment of time. In that instant, we are given citizenship responsibilities by being handed the democratic right to participate in the shaping of our living environment. Observe a public space where there are loose chairs. Almost everyone exercises their rights to move the chairs even if they only move it two inches, and then move it back to where it was.

Environments which contain loose chairs change by the hour. They contain the seeds of their own evolution and generate an ever-varied landscape of infinite combinations. They are therefore infinitely more interesting and lively than over-planned spaces where people are told where they must sit. The chaos that sometimes results from giving people the freedom to fashion their own environment may insult the sensibilities of those who believe that beauty can only be found in total order. I suspect these same people can't wait to escape the mechanized city into the calming embrace of nature — where trees and rocks are never in straight lines or symmetrical designs and where every leaf and snowflake is stamped with its own unique personality.

So bring out those old lounge chairs, kitchen chairs, typist chairs, garden chairs, rocking chairs — paint them if you will — and use them to make *your* street your ever-changing *living* room.

Why not have a chair drive? Ask people to bring out their unused chairs. Have a working bee to fix and paint them. Until street reclaiming becomes a city-wide cultural change, some may go missing. But this is a small price to pay to start reclaiming your street.

ADOPT AN ECCENTRIC

Street reclaiming once again makes room in society for eccentrics, mystics, romantics, artists, and those with a culture different to ours. If eccentrics live in your street or near your street, adopt them as part of your street reclaiming. Create a special place where they can sit and challenge your preconceived ideas. If you don't know any eccentrics, place an advertisement in the local paper: "Wanted: eccentric willing to hang out in our street." Or put a sign on a special seat: "Reserved for eccentrics, mystics, and romantics".

In Praise of Water

There is a strong connection in the human psyche between "water" and "home." Some conjecture this is because we evolved from the sea. Others say it has to do with the fact that we spent the first nine months of our existence nurtured in a sea of water. Whatever the reasons, water has a way of relaxing us and making us feel at home.

Water features prominently in all the world's great streets. And wherever you find water in the street, you find the same activities. Some people will be deep in reflection, carried into a different world on the sound of the running water. Invariably they are oblivious to everything else around. One can only conjecture that when it comes time to think a problem through, many people find the sound of running water to be the voice of a sage. There is wisdom in the chaotic babbling. Others will be letting the water run through their hands. Others will have taken off their shoes and be dangling their feet in the water. There is something comforting and soothing about the feel of running water. Often there will be children playing and splashing in the water. And often adults will slip back into a second childhood and also romp and splash in the water. Water has a way of bringing out the playful child.

Consider integrating water into your street reclaiming works. Start with a kid's wading pool in the centre of the street, surrounded by some deck chairs and a beach umbrella. Create a water feature with a small pond and water pump.

Water. Mysterious, compelling. We have an atavistic need to participate in and with it. In its natural forms, it has enormous raw emotional content. Of all materials available to the designer, water comes closest to being a universal source of pleasure. Ada Louise Huxtable has written: "Its deeper implications suggest evanescent joys, cleansing of the spirit, the transience of perfection, the insubstantiality of dreams, the flowing continuity of life, and a consummate, fleeting beauty — impermanent, like all great romantic beauties, and therefore more beautiful than the tangible and real ... its pleasures are visual and auditory ... it is a performance and a show. Its playful, changeable range runs from the breathtakingly theatrical to the mysteriously subtle. It is capable of broad jokes and tenuous elegancies. Above all, it is an unparalleled instrument of grandeur and romance.

David Kenneth Specter, *Urban Spaces*

In Praise of Movement, Colour, and Change

Things that are colorful and move attract drivers' attention and create a sense of life in a space. Use the wind and sun to best advantage.

It is also important to understand that when street changes are first introduced, drivers slow down because they are unsure of how they should conduct themselves in the "new" space. However, as time goes on and they become accustomed to the new layout, their speed creeps up. I think that from the perspective of getting motorists to act as guests the most successful street reclaiming strategies will be those that are not static but ever-changing. This is why psychological reclaiming is fundamentally more important than physical reclaiming. Human activity constantly changes the street dynamics. However, I think this principle of change can also be built into physical reclaiming. For example, rather than cementing chairs in the ground, have chairs that people can move. Instead of having permanent art works, have art works that children or residents change. Instead of permanent facilities, have flexible spaces in which activities may change on a regular basis: barbecue one weekend, outdoor table tennis the next, an art display after that. It may even be possible to have some landscaping on wheels — or have it designed so it can be moved with a forklift — so the entire layout of the street can be changed.

Someone's bird aviary could be carried into the street for a couple of weeks.
Turn it into an art installation with a wheel-chair.

Get one or more store-dummies, paint them, and lay them on the sidewalk or in the street.

A dragon can be created by kids for a street celebration and then be left in a car park space. Once a week, it could be moved to different places in the street.

In Praise of Sensuality

Our culture has downgraded sensuality to something smutty. But it once meant a stimulation of the senses. A strawberry is sensual. A seat can be sensual. And a street can be sensual and contain a multitude of sensual experiences.

Sensuality is the ability to feel, touch, smell, hear, and see. Sensuality is the ability for this sensory input to evoke within us an emotional response. Sensuality is nature's greatest gift to us, for it is the doorway through which we experience worlds outside our own. It is the raw material from which our brains fashion new creative products.

Sensuality is the very essence of life. The simplest organisms rely upon it to grow, adapt, and reproduce.

Turn your street into one of the world's great sensual experiences.

City fathers were once unafraid to include the sensuous or even the erotic into public space. This fountain in Bologna, Italy, is watched over by a Pope who is blessing the square.

In Praise of Humor

Humor, according to writers such as Edward deBono and Koestler, was one of the giant leaps forward in the evolution of the human brain. According to Koestler, it signalled the birth of human creativity:

> Thus laughter rings the bell of man's departure from the rails of instinct; it signals his rebellion against the single-mindedness of his biological urges, his refusal to remain a creature of habit, governed by a single set of "rules of the game" (*The Act of Creation*, p.64).

Seen as frivolous by our current culture, humor is one of the foundation stones of creativity and has its own internal logic. The Jester is still the brother of the Sage. By ridiculing King Reason, the Jester allows us to see the world through new eyes and returns us to a world of innocence where anything is possible.

Include humor in your street and you will help unshackle the creativity that has become chained by the serious world of grown-ups.

DANCE STAGE

If there is to be dancing in the streets, a stage may help. Now what else could you use a stage for?

In Praise of Multiple Functions

Try to design all elements so they have multiple functions rather than singular ones. For example, the car sculpture arrangement introduced earlier (see p.104) creates a pinch-point to slow traffic; visually narrows the street; sends a message about the place of cars in the street; provides a protected parking space for a car; and, when not used as a carpark, provides a "secret space" for children. Another example is the creation of what I call "multi-use bays" (see drawing below). Landscaping is used to create a protected bay which can be used for end-in parking or for community activities such as a barbecue, table-tennis tournament, bike maintenance clinic, birthday party, etc. Temporary parking arrangements are made for these events (someone's driveway or backyard). The multi-use bay is inherently flexible because it is not over-designed. It is left as a blank canvas upon which the community can create its own meaning over and over again — much as the children can do with their rocks in the Boulder mall.

The multi-use bay can be used for parking cars, for a street barbecue, a table tennis tournament, a bike maintenance clinic, children's play, etc. It is left as a blank canvas for the community to design its own activities.

Building multiple functions into spaces creates a greater density of social and cultural activity. For example, when building the street reclaiming model used to create some of the drawings in this book, I was developing the market-garden layout and decided it should have roadside stalls. But a traditional market garden stall may only get used once a month. By changing the design and creating the shade structure shown on the page opposite, I ended up with a device that could generate street activity every day while still fulfilling the original function I had in mind. It provides shade for parked cars; visually narrows the street; provides a part ceiling; can be used as a picnic table; provides a shady spot for someone to sit and read, write, do homework or office work, or converse or it can be used as a produce stall on market weekends. It is this density of activity that will bring your street alive. As a bonus, density of activity will also help to slow down traffic.

However, one must always remember that people must be allowed to make a space their own, which means adapting it to their particular needs (see Removing the Machine Stamp, p.117).

In Praise of Facilities that Generate Income

Many streets are wide enough to include facilities or activities — corner store, telecommute cottage, coffee shop (see next page), farmers' market (see below), artisans market, etc. — that could generate income which could pay for reclaiming work. Following examples from Europe, you could even build an archway entry that contains the gatekeeper's quarters or a corner store.

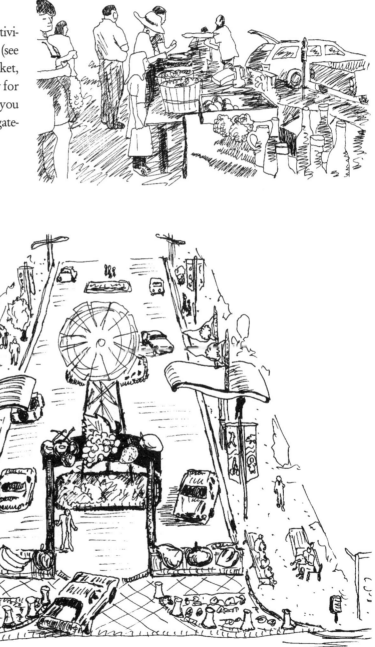

Many streets in Australia, the USA, Canada, and the UK are wide enough to include a range of commercial facilities while still allowing traffic flow.

In Praise of Slow, Organic Reclaiming

In *Reclaiming Our Cities and Towns (Towards an Eco-City)*, I described how our scientific, mechanistic mode of thinking has impacted on the way we design our cities. For example, streets are seen as giant machines for moving traffic, and the job of the engineer is to optimize the efficiency of this traffic-moving machine. One result of this is that we think the solution to every problem lies in a "hardware" item: a wider street, a channelized intersection, coordinated traffic lights, light-rail, a bikeway, etc. Yet more often than not, solutions lie in changing the *relationship* between *existing* parts — what I call "software" solutions. Let me illustrate.

In the Paris street scene below, we have some people drinking coffee and people-watching. In workshops I do with planning professionals, I ask them what the design elements in this space are that facilitate the people-watching exchange. They will come up with a whole range of answers. The seats are arranged like seats in a theatre giving people permission to watch the drama played out in the faces of the passerby. The buildings hem the space in, creating a stage — if there were large carparks in front of the buildings and the buildings were set back, there would be no sense of stage. The shops and the apartments above the shops generate the actors for the stage. Car traffic has been removed, which allows the actors to take center stage. There is a degree of ambiguity — there is no clear definition of where the road ends and the sidewalk

A castle, made of cartons, rocks, and old branches, by a group of children for themselves, is worth a thousand perfectly detailed, exactly finished castles, made for them in a factory.

Christopher Alexander, *Pattern Language*

The most lively and famous streets, it can be observed, are not "developed," "built" or "made." They evolved, resisting cataclysmic change, withstanding fads, adapting incrementally and clinging to the character of place.

Roberta Brandes Gratz, *The Living City*

Too many pedestrian malls and redone streets are over-designed. There's too much unified signage, too many award-winning light standards — too much good taste in general, or the pretensions of it, and since many designers have the same good taste, the result is bland conformity.

William Whyte, *City*

begins or where public space ends and private space begins. There is a high density of doorways and windows, which seduces the pedestrians to keep walking by offering them glimpses into another world at regular intervals. The street is curved, preserving something of the mystery of what may lie just around the corner. I then ask these planning professionals which of these design elements they think is the crucial one, and they will argue back and forth why the one they nominated is the key. It is then that I explain that it is not any one single element in the picture that facilitates the people-watching exchange, but rather the *relationship* between these elements. In other words, lining chairs up in a straight line in the middle of a desert does not guarantee that a people-watching exchange will take place. It is not the chairs per se, but the relationship these chairs bear to the other elements.

To illustrate this point, I use the scene of two men playing chess on a retaining wall around a tree in Fremantle, in Western Australia (see below.) I ask them to imagine that this retaining wall was made a foot higher or a foot lower and to imagine

what would change in the picture. They imagine that the two men would no longer be playing chess on the wall. They imagine that the third man watching them would not stay there staring at a blank wall. They imagine the other people sitting on the wall in the background would also disappear. They then imagine that other people would not feel as comfortable in this space because it is the presence of other people that makes spaces feel both interesting and safe. So by changing one small element in the picture, the whole dynamics of how this space works as a people-space may be changed.

Now what is interesting is that spaces like the Paris street scene have evolved organically over centuries. Someone did not sit down and create a masterplan for a space that facilitates people-watching. If there ever was a master plan, its original purpose has been long forgotten and subverted. (In fact, in Paris the boulevards were masterplanned as a way of suppressing political dissent.) The relationship between the various elements of this environment is something that has changed and evolved — and will continue to evolve. There is therefore inherent in a space like this the same kind of aesthetic pleasure we get from looking at a tree, mountain range, or rocky headland. Chaotic forces have miraculously created meaning and shape — a meaning and shape that has personality and character. Spaces that are master-designed and built in a day have a machine stamp that obliterates personality and character. This machine stamp can only be removed as people commit sacrilege and use the space for purposes for which it was not originally designed. In so doing, they remove the machine stamp and impart their own personality and character to the space.

I therefore find myself loath to encourage residents to masterplan their street reclaiming works. And that is why I continually underline the point that psychological reclaiming is both the starting point and the crucial form of reclaiming. Once residents have psychologically reclaimed their street, they will naturally move on to take back some of the physical space. Yet offering them the opportunity of taking back physical space is important in changing their psychological attitude toward their street.

The answer, I believe, is to encourage residents to take the physical reclaiming slowly and to allow it to emerge organically. I think that creation of blank spaces such as the multi-use bays, or simply marking out a space with some bollards and road paint and calling it a "community meeting point" are ways in which residents can "grow" their own reclaiming works. These blank canvases become something upon which they can evolve the layout organically.

There is a quality even meaner than outright ugliness or disorder, and this meaner quality is the dishonest mask of pretended order, achieved by ignoring or suppressing the real order that is struggling to exist and to be served.

Jane Jacobs, *The Death and Life of Great American Cities*

FIREPIT

Fire. Toasted marshmallows. Tall tales. Ah, the magic of a camp fire ... in the middle of your street.

REMOVING THE MACHINE STAMP

Someone once said that a space does not become a place until it is used for a purpose not intended by the designer. This principle is summed up in this picture. Instead of using the Council-provided exercise equipment to exercise, this lady is doing the exact opposite and using it to relax. In so doing, she is removing the machine stamp of the designer and making herself at home.

USE THE CROSSROADS

In studying pedestrian behavior in New York, William Whyte discovered that most conversations occurred at street corners. Start your reclaiming on a corner. It is guaranteed to generate more activity.

Beg For, Borrow, or Buy Your Own Materials

I encourage neighborhoods to beg, borrow, or buy their own materials for street reclaiming and where possible to do their own construction and maintenance. Works may be done in partnership with council, but I would prefer to see neighborhoods take a few years to finish their street reclaiming than to have the works paid for and completed by council.

My reasons for this are fourfold:

1. Goodwill infrastructures and the collective enterprise. As noted earlier, many of the most promising traffic reduction technologies are based on reciprocating for mutual benefit. These require what I call "goodwill infrastructure" — the opportunity for people to work together and put effort into the collective enterprise. Goodwill infrastructure is like money; the more you invest it, the more you get back. This is what Chris Cunningham calls the "altruistic surplus" of a city: what citizens are willing to put into the collective enterprise above what they draw out. The most livable cities are those with the highest altruistic surplus or goodwill infrastructure. People feel good about participating in the collective enterprise and are willing to go the extra mile to make it work better. In turn, everyone benefits from this goodwill infrastructure which provides a supportive, nurturing environment. Because governments have always been hung up on hardware items to solve every problem, they have ignored the city's most basic resources for solving problems: the creative power of residents and goodwill infrastructure. Evidence from the first round of trials of the *Traffic Reduction Kit* is that people are willing to make an investment in

An old boat in someone's back yard could be placed in a parking bay and converted into play equipment.

this goodwill infrastructure if the right conditions are created. Getting neighborhoods to work on implementing their own street reclaiming, I believe, is an essential step in building the goodwill infrastructure so that other traffic reduction strategies such as the Walking Bus and Car Sharing Clubs become viable.

2. People's commitment to cultural change. I believe that resident ownership of the street reclaiming process is essential in cementing in place the commitment people make to reducing their car use. These reclaiming works, established by the residents' own sweat, will be a permanent reminder of the commitment they made to reduce their own car use and to act as guests in other people's streets. If these works are paid for and implemented by an anonymous someone else, then the whole message of taking personal responsibility is weakened.

A table tennis table could be sponsored by a local shop.

3. Equity and the democratic process. My third reason for arguing that residents should do their own street reclaiming has to do with equity and the redemocratization of our society. The loss of the street as the epicenter of community life undermines the democratic process and leads to the centralization of power and the creation of elites. As noted earlier, the street is the birthplace and sustainer of the democratic process. If we as a society are truly committed to democracy, we need to give back to our streets their role as primary centres of governance. This must start with the very design of the street space.

4. Aesthetics and the sense of home. Works that are paid for and completed by council are also designed by council. These traditional traffic calming works have an engineering focus and are designed according to preset "rules." This usually results in a machined environment lacking any character or personality. All calmed streets in a particular city look alike. This undermines both the aesthetics of the street and the sense of home for residents.

The secular fabric of the medieval town in Europe was organic, subtle and even democratic. Imbued with classical ideas of proportion and layout borrowed largely from Vitruvius, nineteenth century architectural theorists tended to regard medieval townscapes as chaotic and haphazard. The view is far from the truth. There is order in these towns but it is the order of community rather than of individual will. The relationship between public space and private buildings is such as to make spaces lively, useful, and aesthetically satisfying.

Chris Cunningham and Martin Auster, *Urban Design and Regulation*

Suggested Design 'Rules'

Don't use devices which are exclusively a traffic disincentive

Use nothing which is purely a disincentive to traffic. Everything must have an aesthetic or amenity function. While elements may be arranged in a way that slows traffic, the primary function of the element itself must be to improve the social, cultural, or economic life of the neighborhood. Speed bumps are therefore not acceptable because they focus on punishing drivers and do not have a direct amenity function. Instead, create such a positive and lively environment in your street that drivers will *want* to slow down to absorb the ambience. Distract them with life-enhancing action and art. Seduce them into going slower rather than beating them with a stick.

Try to avoid traffic-oriented devices

Reduce to an absolute minimum traffic-oriented devices such as official signage, straight white lines, and concrete islands. Instead use banners, sculptures, and the general layout of the street to convey your message. The kid's trike mounted on a post will say far more than an official sign saying "Warning-Kids at Play." Traffic-oriented devices reinforce the message that the space is primarily one for traffic. This is one of the central problems with traffic calming as currently practiced. The result is an engineered environment that still looks like a space primarily for cars — an obstacle course to challenge driving skills. The goal of street reclaiming is to change the feel of the street

Messages can be conveyed in the design of banners and sculptures.

so it feels less like a car environment and more like an outdoor living room. People don't put "Keep Left" or "Keep Right" signs on their furniture. Flow patterns are self-evident by the very layout of the furniture.

Don't banish cars

The problem is not cars. The problem is too many cars going too fast. Cars going at an appropriate speed can actually enhance the perceptions of action in a space, making it more interesting and safe. So welcome cars as guests into your outdoor living room.

Integrate those "at the margins"

As noted earlier, much design alienates those "at the margin" — in particular children, the elderly, those with disabilities, and so-called eccentrics. The loss of the street for spontaneous exchange has hit these groups hardest. Any design should therefore focus on making sure these people are integrated into community life, rather than being further alienated. I believe that the success of any street reclaiming should be measured by how well it integrates those "at the margins." This is yet another argument for not overplanning your street reclaiming works. Let those "at the margin" come up with the details by providing them with a blank canvas on which they can design their space through use.

The success of any street reclaiming will be judged by how well it helps integrate those who are most easily marginalized in society.

Street reclaiming should unlock the playful and creative child in us all.

The street must once again become the cradle of great civilizations.

It is possible that the great innovators of architecture in our time will not be form-givers at all, but those who invent political and procedural techniques for making effective design possible

Robert L Durham quoted in Jan Tanghe et al, *Living Cities*

How Street Reclaiming differs from Traffic Calming

Traffic calming has come to mean the placement of physical devices in the road to force traffic to slow down (not what I intended when I wrote *Traffic Calming*). By making it difficult to drive down the street, traffic calming strategies aim to force traffic to use major roads. The spirit of street reclaiming can be better understood by comparing these two different approaches.

- The **major focus** of traffic calming (TC) is to slow down traffic. The major focus of street reclaiming (SR) is to convert street space into places for social and cultural exchange. Where appropriate, SR uses the same ways of changing street geometry to slow traffic as TC, but it does not rely solely on this technique. However, the slowing of traffic is viewed as a means to an end — *making the street work as a space for other social and cultural activities.*

- The **primary technique** used by TC is to change the geometry of the street. While SR changes the geometry (where appropriate), it focuses more on changing the psychological feel of the street so that drivers feel like they are driving through someone's outdoor living room. Thus SR can be used on major roads where the range of TC techniques is much more limited.

- The TC **approach** is based on *disincentives* for motorists to speed while SR is based on *incentives:* incentives for people to walk and cycle, thus reducing overall traffic levels; and incentives for motorists to drive slower by giving them more interesting environments with which to engage when passing through the street.

- In street reclaiming, residents design, source materials, build, and maintain works. Therefore residents have a much higher level of **initiative and control** in SR than with TC. This is to promote a stronger sense of community and to increase the sense of responsibility for solutions to both local and city-wide traffic problems.

- The **covert message** of TC is that other people cause traffic problems and that they can be only dealt with in a punitive fashion. The covert and overt message of SR is that residents must accept responsibility for their part in traffic problems and that they cannot ask others to modify their behavior if they don't also modify their own.

chapter four

Six Weeks To Less Traffic

A Practical Program

Introducing the Traffic Reduction Treaty

In the previous chapters, I have presented two new concepts: *traffic reduction* and *street reclaiming*. But these concepts alone will not help you take back your street. This chapter explains a practical way of *applying* these concepts (as used in the *Traffic Reduction Kit* — see www.lesstraffic.com). Stage one takes about six weeks and can be undertaken without any assistance from the local authority. It is a fun, celebratory low-tech approach which does not require ongoing committees or high levels of organization. This is certainly not the only way to apply traffic reduction and street reclaiming principles, but it does offer one immediate way that ordinary citizens can take action to reclaim their streets.

To make the traffic reduction and street reclaiming ideas more concrete, the *Traffic Reduction Kit* gets the residents in a street to sign and exchange a *Traffic Reduction Treaty*. These streets are known as *Traffic Reduction Treaty Streets*.

The idea for the treaty came from an observation. I travel widely, and in every city I have found the same story. *Everyone* wants less traffic in *their* street. And *everyone* wants the traffic to go slower in *their* street. I have never yet met anyone campaigning for more or faster traffic.

So if everyone wants less traffic and slower traffic, the solution seems self-evident. Why not get streets to sign a treaty with each other. A gentleperson's agreement: We will put less traffic in your street, and act as guests when driving in your neighborhood, if you put less traffic in our street and act as guests when driving in our neighborhood.

Such a *Traffic Reduction Treaty* would tackle the root-causes of traffic problems, and not just treat the symptoms. *Everyone* has had their quality of life diminished by excessive traffic — even those who live in quiet cul-de-sacs or on traffic-calmed streets. We are all forced to breathe poisoned air; to endure noise and fumes when shopping; to send our kids to schools located on major roads; to be mired in traffic congestion; to become a full-time chauffeur to our children; to drive more than we need because public transport is inadequate; or to take our life in our hands every time we want to walk or cycle. And as I argued in the first chapter and in my previous books, our entire society has paid a very high social and cultural price for the loss of the street as the epicenter of community life.

What is needed in our cities, therefore, is a new way of dealing with traffic problems. This will not happen while we simply blame others for traffic problems or apply band-aids like traffic calming. Some neighborhoods need to show a better way to a better future.

Traffic Reduction TREATY

In recognition of the rights
of ALL citizens to:
• clean air
• a safe environment for children
• quality urban environments
we hereby commit ourselves to:

1 Reduce our car use
and put less traffic
in each other's street

2 Reduce our speed
and act like a guest
in each other's neighborhood

3 Reclaim the space we save
to improve the social, cultural
and economic life of
our neighborhoods and city

4 Convince other
streets to sign
this treaty.

✓ Less Traffic
✓ Slower Speed
✓ Better Neighbourhoods

Come to the Party

Like recent changes in attitudes to smoking, the *Traffic Reduction Treaty* promotes a new respect for the rights of others. The preamble of the treaty reads: "In recognition of the rights of ALL citizens to clean air, a safe environment for children, and quality urban environments, we hereby commit ourselves to ...."

The starting point for any long-term solution to traffic problems must be an acknowledgement that, while car movement bestows some benefits on those inside the car, it has negative impacts on those outside the car. If you think about how other people's car use erodes your quality of life, you need to accept that your car use is similarly eroding other people's quality of life. The extent to which our car use impacts negatively on the neighborhoods we pass through can be mitigated, just as smokers may continue to smoke but modify their behavior to reduce the impact on others.

In the next chapter I will explore why traffic is a "collective phenomenon" (something which is greater than the sum of its parts) which cannot be adequately addressed by appealing to individuals to take a unilateral decision for the good of the city. Most people suspect that their sacrifice will simply free up road space for others to act irresponsibly. The *Traffic Reduction Treaty* is therefore a mechanism for facilitating a collective solution to something which is a collective problem.

The idea of a *Traffic Reduction Treaty* had its genesis during the community battle against Route 20 in Brisbane in 1987. As a member of CART (Citizens Against Route 20, later changed to Citizens Advocating Responsible Transportation), I argued very strongly that we should take the moral high ground and not try and push the problem into someone else's back yard. Instead we looked for, and advocated, city-wide and long-term solutions. In spite of having no previous interest in transport or urban design issues, quickly I realized that we as residents were part of the problem. Much of the traffic on Route 20 was not cross-town traffic but residents making short trips to drop kids at school or to go to the local shops. I therefore advocated an idea which was not picked up at the time — the idea of a contract with government in which we undertook to reduce the amount of traffic we as a community generated in return for a "calming" of Route 20 rather than an "upgrade."

I have remained convinced that local solutions to traffic problems must be devised within the context of city-wide solutions. And herein lies the problem with traffic calming as currently practiced. It is a localized response to a city-wide problem which does not address the root cause of traffic problems: too much traffic going too fast in the entire system. Traffic

calming carries a covert message: It is other people who cause traffic problems. Traffic calming tries to address the traffic problem in a particular street by throwing some bricks or speed bumps in the way of the traffic.

Now this does not mean that I am not sympathetic to those whose street is clogged with "rat-runners" avoiding major roads. It is even legitimate for the people on these streets to say that it is other people who are causing the traffic problems on their street. But this ignores the fact that when the people who live on this rat-run street drive their cars, they probably do to others what others are doing to them.

Some people may counterargue that what traffic calming is doing is simply forcing traffic back onto major roads where it rightfully belongs. But this also ignores the fact that major roads are where other people live (often elderly or poorer people), where everyone shops, and where most schools are located. I strongly reject the notion that some streets are for living and others are for driving. It is true that some streets must carry more traffic than others. But because of the historical development of our cities, major arterials are also part of our living fabric. Simply diverting traffic out of some streets and concentrating them on major arterials does not address the fundamental issue of how this extra traffic on the major arterials directly undermines the livability for the residents there as well as for those who shop, work, recreate, or go to school on these roads.

Like recent changes in attitudes to smoking, Traffic Reduction Treaty Streets respect the rights of others to quality urban environments.

The residents of this street in Sydney have begun reclaiming their street by building a mobile coffee bar which they wheel out into the street on sunny weekend days.

I hear some people living on rat-run streets — particularly in the inner city — saying, "Yes, but it is the people who live on their acreages on the outskirts of town that are causing our problem. We don't drive past their house but they drive past ours." Again there is some validity in this argument. But the way you get these people to modify their behavior is not by throwing bricks and speed bumps. What is needed, first and foremost, is a city-wide cultural change where everyone reduces their car use to an absolute minimum and everyone respects the neighborhoods through which they drive. Once this cultural change is in place, the quality of transport options will increase and the people in outer suburbs will have viable alternatives.

At best, traffic calming fiddles at the edges of the problem. It does not go to the heart of the problem. What is needed is neighborhoods willing to take moral leadership and actually to tackle the root causes of traffic problems. I believe this book proves that such neighborhoods do not need to make a huge sacrifice in taking such leadership. Leadership has its rewards — in this case, not only savings in time and money for the households in the neighborhood, nor just the long-term reduction in volume and speed of traffic on the streets, nor just the satisfaction of being part of a city-wide cultural change. The ultimate benefit is the reclaiming of the street as the epicenter of social, cultural, and economic activity.

OUR SPLIT PERSONALITY

As a 'driver' speed is important

As a 'resident' speed is a curse

We are in our 'driver' persona, where speed is valued, for one hour per day

We are in our 'resident' or 'consumer of urbanity' persona, where speed is a curse, for 23 hours a day.

Treaty Commitments

Traffic Reduction Treaty Streets make four basic commitments when they sign the treaty:

Commitment 1: Reduce our car use and put less traffic in each other's street. It is important to underline that this does not necessarily mean that people have to forego something to reduce their car use. Just as reducing trash does not mean asking people to eat less, traffic reduction does not mean going without the necessities and luxuries of life.

Commitment 2: Reduce our speed and act like guests in other people's neighborhoods. In the early development of the *Traffic Reduction Kit*, residents and councils worldwide told me that the Kit had to address the issue of speed. Speed, even more than volume of traffic, is what erodes quality of life.

Reducing our speed requires a very simple change in mental attitude. We all have a split personality when it comes to speed. For drivers, speed is of utter-most importance. We want to get from point A to Z as quickly as possible and woe betide any slow-coach that gets in our way. Half a millisecond becomes a matter of life and death. Yet when we get out of the car at the end of the journey and want to cross the road to a park with our child, other people's speed becomes a curse. When we want to drink coffee at an outdoor coffee shop or hold a conversation with someone over the front fence, other people's speed is a curse. In our

Traffic Reduction Treaty Streets will become the premier addresses in a city because they will exhibit a stronger sense of community and have a stronger local economy, better overall amenity, and a vibrant street life.

"motorist" persona we highly value speed. In our "resident" or "consumer of urbanity" persona speed is a curse because it destroys amenity.

We spend on average about one hour per day in our "motorist" persona. For the other 23 hours we are in our "resident" persona where speeding traffic erodes amenity. As a society, we must confront this internal dilemma and find a better balance. When driving, we must find ways of calming the raging motorist within ourselves. Recognizing the impact that our speeding has on the neighborhoods through which we pass is the first step.

I remember when this truth first dawned on me. During the Route 20 "freeway" fight in Brisbane (the baptism of fire that first got me interested in traffic and city design,) I was confronted with how traffic was already affecting residents' social and cultural life. People told me stories of how street life had changed as traffic had increased. Suddenly I could no longer drive anywhere without thinking about the impact that my driving was having on others. I decided to drive 20 kilometres an hour below the speed limit. This proved very difficult at first because the "motorist" in my head (not to mention the motorists behind me) would become incredibly impatient. But I found that this decision changed my whole perspective on the notion of speed.

Commitment 3: Reclaim the space we save to improve the social, cultural, and economic life of our neighborhood and city. As mentioned already, if residents reduce their car use, valuable road and carparking spaces city-wide are saved. In their own street, residents should be given back this space they have saved as a reward for their reduced car use. It is important to stress that this saved space should be reused immediately. As mentioned earlier, if it is not reused, it will simply encourage other people to make inefficient transport choices. The long-term result would be a shuffling of inefficiencies in the transport system rather than their elimination.

Commitment 4: Convince other streets to sign this treaty. It is obvious that the greater the number of streets in a city that become *Traffic Reduction Treaty Streets*, the greater the rewards for everyone. Therefore, one of the commitments of a *Treaty Street* is to convince others that they should also do the right thing and sign the treaty.

However, I believe that residents will be motivated to become *Treaty Streets* not just because of the negative motivation of wanting to reduce traffic. *Traffic Reduction Treaty Streets* will become the premier addresses in a city because they will exhibit a stronger sense of community and have a stronger local economy, better overall amenity, and a vibrant street life.

How the Traffic Reduction Treaty works for one family

At the Traffic Reduction Treaty Street Party, the Witmores worked out a plan to reduce their car use...

Daddy Witmore started taking the bus to work.

The little Witmores got the Walking Bus to school ... even on rainy days.

The Witmores shopped locally.
(Billy Witmore eventually got a job at the local Deli. Daddy Witmore said he never dreamed that shopping locally would buy one of his kids a job!)

Eventually the Witmores sold their car and joined a Car Share Club.

They had some great holidays with all the money they saved on car use.

And their street, which was once a speed track, was now a nicer place to live.

PHASE ONE *(six weeks)*

1. GETTING STARTED
• *Personal preparation*
• *Form Interim Organizing Group*
•*Stir curiosity*
•*Household visit*

2. EDUCATING RESIDENTS

3. VOTING ON BECOMING TREATY STREET

4. STREET PARTY
• *Sign and exchange Treaty*
• *Traffic reduction plan for households*
• *Traffic reduction plan for street*
• *Begin Psychological Reclaiming*
• *Ideas for Physical Reclaiming*

5. TRIAL WEEK
• *Expand Psychological Reclaiming*
• *Implement Reduction Plans*
• *Measure reduced car use*

6. EVALUATION

PHASE TWO *(ongoing)*

7. EXTEND PSYCHOLOGICAL RECLAIMING

8. MENTOR OTHER TREATY STREETS

9. PHYSICAL RECLAIMING

10. MUTUAL BENEFIT SCHEMES

Overview of Process

What follows is a practical program to reclaim your street. A more detailed description of how each element can be implemented can be obtained from www.lesstraffic.com. The elements do not necessarily have to follow the order laid out here. If you make improvements to the process, please let me know via the web site so they can be shared with others.

I have broken the program into two distinct phases. The goals for each phase are the following:

Phase One (takes around six weeks) —

• Educate residents about *traffic reduction*, the *Traffic Reduction Treaty* and *street reclaiming*

• Vote on becoming a *Traffic Reduction Treaty Street*

• Sign and exchange the treaty with another street

• Develop a traffic reduction plan for each household and the street

• Try out and measure the effectiveness of the reduction plan

• Psychologically reclaim your street

Phase two (ongoing) —

• Extend psychological reclaiming

• Physically reclaim your street if appropriate

• Mentor other *Traffic Reduction Treaty Streets* and exchange treaties

• Reciprocate for mutual benefit with other *Treaty Streets*.

The process has been broken into two phases so that your street gets a sense of accomplishment early in the process. Phase One does not require any complicated negotiations with council and can be done relatively quickly. Phase Two may require negotiations and will definitely take longer than Phase One. If you only complete Phase One, or even if you only get part way through it, you will have made a very valuable contribution to changing car culture in your city. The residents in your street will view their street differently and even subconsciously begin psychologically to reclaim it. This will eventually lead to physical changes in your street.

Phase One

1. Getting started

Personal preparation: Educate yourself as much as possible about the concepts in this book. If possible, visit www.lesstraffic.com and order any other educational materials available. Reread this book until you feel like you have a firm grasp of the concepts. This will help you be more effective and avoid some of the pitfalls.

Contact your council to see what support they offer to streets wanting to become *Traffic Reduction Treaty Streets*. Your council may have resources such as the *Traffic Reduction Kit* that they make available to streets like yours.

Contact other streets in your neighborhood or city that have been through this process. council may provide this information or you may find it on the Web site.

Form Interim Organizing Group: You only need one person to start this process — you. Get one or two other people in your street who you know are concerned about traffic, and ask them if they will help you organize a six-week program to reclaim your street. Lend them the educational material you have got, or invite them to your house to view a video like *Less Traffic, Slower Speed: How the Traffic Reduction Treaty Works*. If you don't know whether any of your neighbors are concerned, knock on their door and ask them if they are concerned about the impact of traffic on their quality of life.

The *Interim Organizing Group* need only get the ball rolling. Once the rest of the street has been exposed to the ideas, they should decide whether to proceed and volunteer to help organize the rest of the program.

Define area to be covered by scheme: The first thing for the organizing group to decide is the households that will be included in the initial scheme. This process works best if you keep the number as small as possible. I strongly suggest that this be a single street for a single block. Anything larger and you have to coordinate too many people. This is also the ideal outer boundary for creating a single "outdoor living room." You could choose a smaller area if you have a very long block and there is some feature which divides it into two or more rooms — for example, a creek, park or, bend in the road. You can choose a larger area if your block is very small or there is a small pocket of houses that connect to your street.

Some people may argue that everyone in the larger street or neighborhood is affected by traffic and should be involved from the start. The beauty of this process is

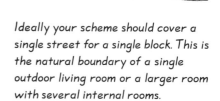

Ideally your scheme should cover a single street for a single block. This is the natural boundary of a single outdoor living room or a larger room with several internal rooms.

that it can grow. If you get the people in one block of your street to reduce their car use and to reclaim their street, the people in the next block may want to do the same. In fact, the second phase of this process encourages an active mentoring of other blocks in your street and neighborhood.

Some engineers will respond that calming streets must be done on a precinct basis, otherwise calming one street may simply push traffic onto another parallel street. This is true when streets are relying on council to spend hundreds of thousands of dollars to calm a whole precinct. But this process of street reclaiming is open to anyone willing to make a contribution to tackling the city-wide problem. If reclaiming your street causes traffic to increase on a parallel street, then the people on the parallel street can solve the problem by simply doing what you have done — sign the treaty and reclaim their street. It could even be argued that if some traffic gets displaced into another street this may be something positive that encourages a faster spread of street reclaiming with significant traffic reductions for the entire city.

However, it should be kept in mind that Phase One of the process only deals with *psychological* reclaiming. Phase Two, the physical reclaiming, can be done over a longer period *if needed*. I therefore recommend that the streets in a neighborhood work together in this physical reclaiming phase. That way, measures can be implemented that complement each other and will make sure that one street does not do something to disadvantage others.

Stir curiosity: Erect posters or create chalk messages on the road in your street at the beginning of the process to stir curiosity. You may put up signs like, *Do You Want Less Traffic in this Street? Details Coming Soon.* You can do other things to stir curiosity, like putting up balloons and streamers, creating a display in the back of a trailer, or using a car as a display board.

Household visit: Divide the households in your street amongst the members of the organizing group and visit each household, inviting them to be part of the process. Using a *Household Record Card* for each household will help you keep track of who has got what information. These cards can also be used to compile interesting information about how successful your program has been.

HOUSEHOLD RECORD CARD

Address...

Names..

....

....

....

Phone no...

No. under 13 years of age.......... over 13 years of age.........

No of cars in household ....

☐ Fridge Pouch

Seen video ☐ info night ☐ via Treaty Advocate

Vote to become Treaty Neighborhood ☐ yes ☐ no

Pretreaty car use .... km

☐ Street party invite

Trial week car use .... km

Treaty Advocate
....

OTHER:

2. Educating residents

Education event: Everyone in your street needs to understand the traffic reduction and street reclaiming concepts if they are to vote on becoming a *Traffic Reduction Treaty Street*. One way is for the Interim Organizing Group to hold a viewing of a video like *Less Traffic, Slower Speeds* at someone's house.

If there are a lot of households in your street and you don't have a venue large enough for this "big event" viewing, it can be broken down into a series of smaller viewings. At this viewing, residents should be invited to join the organizing group.

One strategy for ensuring everyone gets exposed to the educational materials is to divide the households in your street amongst the volunteers on the Organizing Group. Ideally each person would have about five households to look after. These *Treaty Advocates* (as I call them) then ensure that the households in their care are exposed to the educational materials and get invitations to events like the street party. In the initial trials, residents highly valued this arrangement for the way it helped build a stronger sense of community and kept the workload on individuals to a minimum.

Compile a list of those who attend this first educational event so that the Treaty Advocates know which of the households in their care have not yet had the opportunity of viewing the video.

You can lend this book to households that are interested in learning more or refer them to the Web site.

Involvement of children: Run a competition in which kids answer these questions either in words or in a drawing:

- How were streets different when your parents were your age? What were they allowed to do that you are not?
- Imagine your street as a Kids' Street. What would you like to see in your street?

The street party is the major activity in this celebratory, community-building approach to reclaiming your street.

3. Voting on becoming a Treaty Street

It is handy to combine the educational process with the opportunity for people to vote on whether the street should become a *Traffic Reduction Treaty Street*.

A ticklish problem with the voting is the question of what percentage of residents you need to become a *Traffic Reduction Treaty Street*. If your council has an active traffic reduction program under way, they should have guidelines for this. I would recommend a 60% support level for becoming a *Treaty Street*, but a higher level for any permanent reclaiming works. These street works should be done by consensus. I think it should be up to the entire street to decide if they should proceed if there are a few obstinate residents who refuse to negotiate. Of course, this process does not preclude any resident from psychologically reclaiming the street, even if becoming a treaty street is voted down.

4. Street party

As you will see from the next chapter, I believe that cultural change happens through celebration and experience-based events. The central activity of Phase One is therefore a street party in which people can experience first hand the reclaiming of their street. For your street party, I strongly suggest you do not go for a street closure. Use half the street, or if it is a major road, just the sidewalk and carparking spaces. It is important to send the message that cars will still be welcome in your street — as long as they behave as guests. The party is the first act of street reclaiming so it must accommodate traffic while still reclaiming the space. The following are some suggested activities for your street party:

Signing and exchanging the treaty: Get everyone to sign the *Traffic Reduction Treaty* and ceremonially exchange the treaty with another street that has also signed it. If you are the first street in your city to sign the treaty, have a representative of council accept your signed treaty — and make sure the media is there to photograph the exchange. You can also ceremoniously erect a *Treaty Post* on your sidewalk or in the centre of the street and attach a plaque bearing the treaty wording. Underneath you can fix a small engraved plate that bears the details of the date and who the treaty was exchanged with. As you convince other streets to become *Treaty Streets* and exchange the treaty with them, add another engraved plate to your post. (Maybe the City could offer an incentive for the street that exchanges the treaty with the most streets!)

You can get children to sign their own treaty in which they agree not to nag their parents to drive them everywhere and to make sure their parents don't speed in other kids' streets (see example next page).

Household Traffic Reduction Plan: Households should be encouraged to devise their own traffic reduction plan. This household reduction plan can be written on a magnetized card which is attached to the fridge or on a card that can be stuck above where the car keys hang. You can set up a table at your street party where people devise their household reduction plan. A *Treaty Advocate* may help them with this process.

Street Reduction Plan: Talk with each other about ways in which you could work together as a street and neighborhood to reduce your car use. Maybe you can share rides for taking kids to sport, or start a Walking School Bus. Maybe someone can act as a home delivery depot. Maybe someone can run a bike maintenance clinic.

---

*Our Household
Reduction Plan*

1. Note all non-urgent trips on fridge organiser
2. Note all shopping needs on fridge organiser
3. John to get bus to work 2 days per week
4. Bill and Sharon to go to school via Walking Bus
5. Walk to church on Sundays
6. Bill to share ride with Johnstones for Judo

THINK BEFORE YOU **DRIVE**

Kids' Traffic BUSTER TREATY

I will work with Walter B. Wombat and other Kids in helping make all streets safer for kids

✔ *I will not nag my parents to drive me everywhere*

✔ *I will help my family use its car less*

✔ *I will help my family drive slower in other Kid's streets*

Signed.....................................

Date...........................

Walter B. Wombat 🐾
Thanks Dude

Kids Traffic Buster Treaty which kids can sign at the Street Party

Ideas for psychological reclaiming: The street party should be the first step in the psychological reclaiming of your street. But you need to decide what to do next. What will individuals do? What is the first street activity? What physical things can you do immediately to psychologically reclaim your street? (See Chapter Three for ideas.)

Ideas for physical reclaiming: You can begin to discuss ideas for the physical reclaiming of your street. But be careful not to get bogged down in this. The goal of Phase One is to reclaim your street psychologically. Chapter Three will help you develop these ideas for physical reclaiming.

Getting people involved: In addition to the above, you can organize a range of social and fun activities. Chalk murals on the road. Street games. Fancy dress. Posters to put on lampposts. One way of getting everyone to participate is to play *Traffic Buster Bingo*. Create "activity stations" at a number of tables. Each activity station has one of the activities explained above (or some of your own). People get a bingo card (see below) and cross off the activities as they complete them. You can offer a prize for the first person completing all activities. I suggest you also have a "second chance lucky draw" box in which people put their completed bingo cards. This encourages people to keep going with the activities after the first person has completed the card.

HOUSEHOLD **Traffic BUSTER BINGO**

Work with the other members of your household to complete all the activities at the Activity Stations.

WIN PRIZES! **You have two chances:**

1. Be first to finish and call out 'Traffic Buster Bingo'
2. Put completed card in the Second Chance Lucky Draw Box.

The owner of this card lives at

Address..

CROSS OFF ACTIVITY STATIONS AS YOU COMPLETE THEM. COMPLETE IN ANY ORDER

1   2   3   4   5   6   7   8   9

SURVEY WEEK START..

SURVEY WEEK END..

1 Minute Car Use Survey

Your street address

☐ Tick here if you have no cars in your household

Include **ALL** cars in your household

CAR 1	CAR 2	CAR 3	CAR 4
CAR MAKE AND MODEL			
ODOMETER READING START OF SURVEY WEEK			
ODOMETER READING END OF SURVEY WEEK			

All information confidential. We will collect this form.

Sample of the Car Use Survey form used to measure reduced car use during a trial week of reduction plans. Before and after surveys are conducted.

Savings Diary

Day and Date _____

TRIP SAVED OR SHORTENED From where to where?	HOW SAVED	BY WHOM	Km SAVED

See back for how to calculate savings

Sub-Total ☐

The alternative to the Car Use Survey. A sample page of a Savings Diary.

5. Trial week

A Trial Week should begin in the week immediately following the street party. Its purpose is to allow people to measure how effective their traffic reduction strategies are and to experiment with reclaiming their street. Continue the celebratory theme established at your street party during by organizing some fun street activities and encouraging people to spontaneously take over the street.

It is important to document how much your street has reduced the traffic it is generating. Reductions achieved during the Trial Week can be used to legitimize physical street reclaiming in Phase Two. The measure of car use is the total kilometres/miles traveled by the vehicles in your street. I suggest this be measured for a week. There are two ways of measuring the success of your program. The first uses a *Car Use Survey* (see example opposite). This survey must be done twice. The first survey establishes a base measure. This base measure survey must be done *before* you become a *Treaty Street* and before you implement your reduction strategies. The second survey is done during the Trial Week.

I suggest you make the beginning and ending of both survey weeks a time that is easy to remember — Sunday night or the evening that people put out their garbage bins. You may like to put up some lamppost reminders or simply write chalk reminders on the roadway on the day the survey starts and ends. You might not get everyone in the street to complete the survey, but be sure to get as many completed forms as possible.

To calculate the total savings for your street, deduct the total distance travelled in the second survey from the distance travelled in the first survey. Be careful that you include only vehicles that were part of both surveys.

The second method of measuring your reduced car use is to have people fill out a *Savings Diary* during the Trial Week. This diary asks them to write down the occasions they would have normally used the car but used a reduction strategy instead. By getting them to also record the distance they did travel in their car during the Trial Week, a percentage saving can be calculated.

The *Savings Diary* is not as accurate as the *Car Use Survey* but has the advantage of speeding up the overall process because it only has to be completed once — during the Trial Week.

6. Evaluation

Invite all the key participants to evaluate and reflect on the success of Phase One. Record the lessons you learnt or the innovations you developed and find a way of sharing this with other streets. This may be done through the Web site, through your council, or in your mentoring of other Treaty Streets.

Begin the psychological reclaiming of your street in a big way during a Trial Week — the week following the Street Party

Phase Two

7. Expanding psychological reclaiming

Psychological reclaiming is the springboard for any physical reclaiming. It should therefore be nurtured with a range of both planned and spontaneous street activities.

One of the secrets of making your street feel more like an outdoor living room than a street is for it to be ever-changing. "New" environments cause motorists to slow down because they are not sure what to expect. The drivers also slow down to absorb this different environment. But as they get to know the environment, they speed up because they know what to expect and there is nothing new to absorb. It is therefore important to make your street "unpredictable." One of the ways of doing this is to have a wide range of human activities taking place in the street.

8. Mentor others' treaty streets

Your street should try to convince the blocks either side and other streets in your neighborhood to sign the treaty. The best advertisement will be the changes in your street. If you want to be proactive, lend your friends this book or the video. Alternatively, you may hold a party in your street where you invite anyone in the neighborhood who is interested in reducing the impact of traffic in their street. You may have an outdoor showing of the video. This party to proselytize other streets could even become a monthly event — a good excuse to reclaim your street in a big way on a regular basis.

9. Implementing your physical reclaiming — slowly

Physical reclaiming requires the following steps:

Demonstrate your reduced car use: This was completed in phase one with the *Car Use Survey* or *Savings Diary*. This proof of reduced car use is crucial in legitimizing your claims to reclaim your street.

Determine the spaces that can be reclaimed: There is no point discussing what you may like to put in your street until you have an idea of what spaces you can reclaim. This depends on your current street width, the role your street plays in the overall city network, your council's technical requirements regarding lane widths, turning radiuses, etc.

As stated earlier, I believe that the design process should be undertaken by the residents of the street. To help facilitate this, I suggest that you find the two people in your street with the strongest technical bents. Appoint them as *Technical Watchdogs*, their role being to check the technical requirements of council and to help advise the street on what spaces can be taken back.

The next step in determining what spaces can be taken back is to get residents to nominate who would be happy to have reclaimed spaces outside their home. Some people may be happy to lose a car parking space and not have it compensated for. Other people may be willing to lose a car parking space as long as it is compensated for further down the street with some end-in parking. Others may be happy to have the parking space converted into a dual purpose space: a space that is used for both parking and a children's hopscotch area, or a fold-down table tennis table, or a market stall once a month.

The *Technical Watchdogs* should then oversee the creation of some scaled maps/ models of the street. I suggest it be done in 1/86th scale which is HO in scaled railway models. This allows you to readily get cars, people and seating from any railway model shop and to include these in your street model. Mark driveways and where people live on this scaled model. Cut the shapes of potentially reclaimed spaces out of coloured card and put them where they may be placed on the street.

Don't be afraid to bargain hard with your council about what spaces may be taken back. Current guidelines may not be up-to-date with the latest developments. Even space on major arterials can be reclaimed (details opposite).

Dream about what kind of facilities you want: Give people a chance to daydream about the kinds of things they may like to see in their reclaimed street: play areas for children, seating, an outdoor chess set, a coffee shop, a gathering point, a market garden, etc. Discuss these ideas and gauge the level of support for various ideas. Some ideas may be immediately impractical due to the amount of space you have for actual reclaiming.

Test the level of support for the various facilities suggested.

Dialogue with adjoining streets: Maybe you can come up with a joint plan — a corner store in one street, a dance stage in another, and a telecommute cottage in another. This way you increase the diversity of facilities that are available.

Decide your interim reclaiming works: As emphasised in the last chapter on design, I believe slow organic evolution of your reclaiming works is more desirable than a "master plan" —

How space can be reclaimed from major four lane arterials — without loosing capacity

1. It is intersection design that determines the carrying capacity of a road.

2. On a major four-lane arterial, you can remove half a lane in both directions mid-block, leaving just two very wide lanes, without affecting the overall carrying capacity. When traffic is light on this modified four-lane road, it is moving fast and the traffic is accommodated easily by the one wide lane.

3. As the traffic volume increases, the traffic naturally slows down as the intersections approach their maximum carrying capacity. Because the traffic is moving slower, it no longer needs such a large buffer around each car, and the traffic automatically starts using the wide lane as two very skinny lanes.

Personal fulfilment arises when an individual experiences as broad or profound a range of civilization as possible and displays great spontaneity and creativity in integrating that experience into his or her own being.

Kenneth Schneider, *On the Nature of Cities*

which usually means one person's dream over everyone else's. It is preferable to paint a square on the road, put up some temporary bollards, put some seats in the square, and call it a "community meeting place" than to master-design some elaborate structure. Let the "community meeting place" evolve from these humble beginnings.

Decorate and evolve your outdoor living room: Using the guidelines in the previous chapter, begin filling in the details of your design — some banners here, a garden there, some hanging sculptures from the tree branches.

Devise an implementation strategy: Let's imagine your street reaches a consensus on some physical reclaiming measure — whether that be a humble community meeting place or a grand arch entrance complete with home delivery depot and artist's loft. Make sure everyone is happy with the plan. You must be able to demonstrate this support to your council.

If your council is a leader in traffic reduction, they will have an established procedure for the approval of street reclaiming plans. You need to find out what this procedure is. If your council does not allow street reclaiming and you have gone through all the above steps, then I suggest you lobby them to change their policy. At the end of the day I believe that some streets in some cities will need to physically reclaim their streets without council approval as the final step in trying to get council to change its policy. If it comes to this, it is absolutely essential that the street has first documented its own reduced car use and that the plans fit the kind of guidelines being used by other councils in other cities. Neighborhoods who try to reclaim their street without reducing their own car use to a minimum have no moral mandate to do so.

10. Reciprocating for mutual benefit

By working with the streets around you that have also become *Traffic Reduction Treaty Streets,* you can now begin to reap even more of the economic, social, and cultural benefits of this scheme. You will reach a critical mass in your neighborhood where the following schemes will become viable (some require more committed streets than others): Walking School Bus; Shop-and-Employ-Locally Incentive Scheme (such as *SmartMove Rewards Card*); Car Sharing Clubs; and universal transit passes. But these are only the tip of the iceberg. As we rediscover the city as a collective enterprise, we will invent a whole range of win-win social and economic arrangements which will make our living environments a joy to inhabit.

chapter five

PRESERVING THE HEART

Eight Myths Exposed

Once Bitten...

In 1989 I wrote *Traffic Calming* which helped spark the traffic calming revolution in many cities in Australia and North America. However, I quickly became very disillusioned because both community activists and engineers alike adopted some of the techniques advocated but abandoned the setting of those techniques. *Traffic Calming* advocated total "mobility management." It argued (as I have in this book) that transport is a cost we pay to get a benefit at the journey's end and that traffic calming should adopt a city-wide approach that minimizes these costs while maximizing access. It even argued that traffic calming techniques should be applied to major roads.

What we got instead were some of the physical changes (speed bumps, speed tables, neck-downs, chicanes) that could be made in so-called "residential" streets while the planning departments continued to construct bigger and better arterials and freeways. We even had the ludicrous situation of cities justifying road expansion as "Traffic Calming," arguing that these bigger roads were needed to accommodate the traffic that had been displaced from the "residential" streets onto the major roads. However, the clear intent of *Traffic Calming* was that *all* roads in the city should be "calmed."

The physical things that could be photographed got adopted, but the underlying principles were ignored and subverted. Given the experience of what happened to the material in *Traffic Calming*, I have included this chapter to try and prevent history repeating itself. I beg you to absorb the spirit of what I have proposed rather than the physical details.

I have organized this material around eight myths and assumptions that currently drive transport planning in most cities. (These are not the same eight myths that appeared in *Traffic Calming*.) By exposing these myths, I hope to show why current approaches to transport planning are not working. It also gives me the opportunity to contrast the approach taken in this book to the traditional approach. I trust this will help you understand more clearly the heart of what I am proposing so that you do not merely implement the suggested physical changes slavishly. As a bonus, you will find that the principles outlined in this chapter apply to many other areas of social and cultural change as well.

*Traffic is not one car on a street.
Just as all drivers are collectively
responsible for the negative impacts
of traffic, so all residents are
collectively responsible to reclaim
their streets.*

Myth 1: Changing Individual Behavior Is the Key to Building a More Efficient Transport System

Ignoring the consequences of reducing traffic

Most approaches to reducing traffic appeal to individuals to "do the right thing" and leave your car at home for the sake of the city and the environment. But this ignores one of the consequences of convincing people to leave their car at home. Imagine that a city is successful in convincing 100,000 people to leave their car at home. What this creates is 100,000 spare spaces on the road network and 100,000 spare carparking spaces at destinations — a free and under-utilized resource. Universal experience is that traffic expands to fill the available road space, whether this spare capacity is created by engineers widening roads or "good citizens" giving up their cars. The spare capacity is seen as a free resource that can be exploited in some way by other users in the system. For example, spare capacity on a freeway may encourage someone from suburb A to apply for a job in suburb Z on the other side of town instead of taking a little more time to find the same job closer to home. (If the freeway was congested, one would think twice and may decide that it is just too much trouble.) A day later someone from suburb Z starts looking for a job, but the one opportunity to work close to home was taken a day earlier by a person commuting from suburb A. This person from suburb Z eventually finds a job in suburb A and the two pass each other twice a day on the freeway. This one inefficiency (termed "cross-commuting") adds about 60% extra traffic to peak hour traffic in Australia's major cities. Spare capacity encourages an increase in these kind of inefficient choices. So convincing 100,000 residents to give up their cars is likely to result in a reshuffling of inefficiencies, not in their elimination.

Traffic as a collective problem

Interestingly, in the Appleyard study, it was discovered that home territory is eroded by an *increase* in traffic volume and speed. A single vehicle proceeding at walking speed will not inhibit the social and cultural life of a neighborhood. It may even enhance it as some kind of novelty. One car alone on a street does not constitute traffic. For traffic, you need at least two cars. But even two cars will not inhibit the social and cultural life of the street. There are therefore critical thresholds at which traffic begins to erode quality of life. Traffic, by definition, is a collection of individual vehicles sharing a common space. It is a *collective phenomenon*. A collective phenomenon is any arrangement in which the whole is greater than the sum of the parts. The degree to which

The embrace of the automobile as a structuring mechanism for cities reveals a misguided infatuation with a device of the late industrial revolution, whose real utility for people is non-urban travel [emphasis added].... Brilliantly promoted by industry and by government programs, and possessing universal allure, the inherent anti-urban qualities of the automobile are still not generally recognized. In America and around the world, planners systematically repeat the drastic mistake of building and rebuilding urban areas for automobiles rather than for people.

Peter Wolf, Roberta Brandes Gratz, in Living Cities

Car traffic is a collective problem that disrupts the social and cultural life of the city. Collective problems require collective solutions.

traffic erodes home territory cannot be calculated by multiplying the amount of erosion caused by one vehicle by the number of vehicles on the street.

Another way to understand how traffic works as a collective phenomenon is to imagine your city as if cars had never been invented. Where currently there are freeways, there are vibrant communities with a wide range of facilities just around the corner. Where there are car parks outside your local shops, there is a richer diversity of shopping and community facilities. Streets are the epicenter of your community and cultural life. In the evening, adults bring their chairs into the street and children play ball among the adults.

Now imagine that you are the very first person faced with the decision as to whether to buy one of these new inventions, the private car. On the surface you would be a fool to turn the offer down. With your car, you will not only have the wonderful convenience inherent in the current city form, but you will have the flexibility to drive to other parts of the city and maybe even to save money on some purchases.

Even if you have a strong social conscience and weigh the impact on others, the purchase still makes sense. One car moving down people's streets will not affect them in any significant way. The kids can still play ball. You can go around them or wait for them to move aside. Your exhaust fumes will be absorbed into the atmosphere and, while unpleasant for a few seconds, will cause no one any significant problems.

But your decision does not take account of what will happen if 500,000 or a million other inhabitants make the same decision. The collective results of these individual decisions will be to alter radically the entire fabric of the city. Some of the convenience and diversity will have to be sacrificed to car parking and freeways.

However, the results of collective choices also rebound on the motorists themselves. Let's go back to imagining you are the first person with a car in the city. As more and more people buy cars and attempt to use the same road space, they begin to impose time delays on each other. When a particular road is at 25% of its maximum capacity, these motorists will impose about a 12% time delay on each other. If more motorists try to use the same road and traffic increases to 50% of maximum capacity, the time delays will jump to 40%. However, if traffic increases to 98% of maximum capacity, each driver will impose on the other a 700% time delay. These massive delays that motorists impose on each other are not the responsibility of any one motorist.

And this is where we run into a significant problem in dealing with traffic. We approach traffic as if it is something that can be addressed through appealing to individuals. However, problems which are the result of collective action need to be solved through collective action. To address the root causes of traffic problems, we must therefore devise *social* mechanisms that help us take *collective* responsibility for what is a *collective* problem. If we do not devise collective solutions, we will simply chase our tail. This does not mean that we should not ask individuals to "do the right thing." But such a request must come within the envelope of a collective strategy that avoids simply reshuffling the inefficiencies and asking one group to make sacrifices so others can expand their inefficient and unsustainable choices.

 MYTH BUSTER *Collective solutions are the key*

> Traffic reduction, the *Traffic Reduction Treaty*, and street reclaiming are all social mechanisms that enable people to take collective responsibility for a problem which is a collective problem and which cannot be adequately addressed by appealing solely to individual action.

**Defining Hardware and
Software Solutions**

Hardware solutions rely on modifying or providing new physical devices: new roads, coordinated traffic lights, new trains, cycle ways.

Software solutions rely on changing the *relationships* between the existing elements of an environment: the way the physical elements relate to each other; the way people relate to the physical elements; and the way people relate to each other.

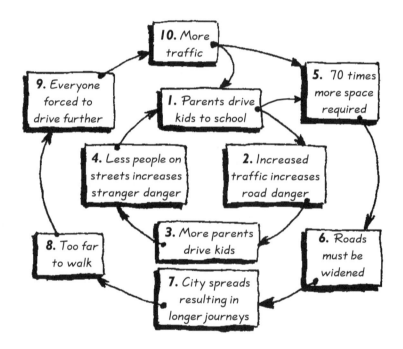

Fig 5.1 A typical negative feedback loop in transport that contains both social/cultural factors and physical environment factors.

Myth 2: Transport Can Be Fixed by Providing New "Hardware" Items

For those who are strongly attached to the car, the hardware items that will solve transport problems are wider roads, freeways, multi-story car parks, tunnels, coordinated traffic lights, and toll-ways. For those who see the car as an enemy, the hardware items that will solve transport problems are light rail, bus ways, integrated ticketing, higher density living, bike ways, and a better walking environment. Both approaches are simplistic because they ignore the fact that transport problems are made up of a complex web of social, cultural, and physical factors. As it turns out, often the place to act first in changing this complex web is *not* with the physical factors. Let me illustrate with a chain reaction set off by one transport decision (Figure 5.1):

1. Imagine that one parent decides to drive his/her child to school.
2. Other parents see the increase in traffic around the school and some judge that it is too dangerous for their kids to walk to school.
3. Some of these parents decide to drive their kids also.
4. Because there are fewer children and parents on the sidewalk walking his/her kids to school, fears of stranger danger increase. So more parents decide to drive their kids to school.

This completes the inner feedback loop.

But this negative cycle feeds into a host of other second-generation cycles. For example:

5. Each time a parent decides to drive his/her child to school, the car trip requires at least 70 times more space to move the child than when they walked.
6. Eventually this means that roads must be widened.
7. This requires the demolition of "destinations" — houses, shops, parks, and other community facilities.
8. The average distance between destinations is increased (a less compact urban fabric.)
9. The number of destinations that can be reached by foot or cycle decreases.
10. Everyone is forced to use the car more.

This completes the inner and outer feedback loops with more parents being forced to drive their kids to school and the demands for more road space increasing. Addressing the root causes of traffic problems requires putting these kinds of negative feedback loops into reverse.

Now what this example illustrates is that at least two of the crucial boxes in these negative feedback loops are social/cultural realities. Perceptions that roads are

We are now desperately short of penetrating concepts to give the city meaningful human context and balance. We do not understand the integration necessary to achieve urban efficiency and urban amenity, to bring nature into the city, or to create satisfying human interaction. What really constitutes urbanity? What is the intellectual or aesthetic or emotional content of a good city? ... While medicine operates with a vision of health, and law with a distant image of justice, city planning exists without such a simple goal.

Kenneth Schneider, *On the Nature of Cities*

too dangerous to let children walk (2) and perceptions of increased stranger danger (4) are social/cultural realities. More often than not, the crucial links in such feedback loops that can be used to reverse the cycle are these social/cultural links.

For example, the above analysis of school traffic led to my inventing the Walking School Bus. The Walking School Bus addresses both social/cultural aspects. The highly coloured trolley enters the roadway before any children and increases the visibility and therefore the safety of children. And by the children walking in an organized group, perceptions of stranger danger are overcome. In addition, the solution is designed to repair some of the damage done by excessive traffic by building a stronger sense of local community and reclaiming the street for walking. The Walking School Bus is not essentially a hardware item (although one may be involved) but a "software solution" relying on creating a social structure.

How our beliefs get built into our streets

In a workshops I do with planning professionals, I ask them to pretend they are anthropologists examining the African tribal compound of the Ambo people (see opposite). I ask them what they can tell me about the beliefs, culture, and mythologies of the Ambo people by looking at this diagram. You may want to do this exercise yourself before reading on.

There is a lot you can tell about the Ambo people by looking at a map of their kraal. They put a high value on cattle — invaders must first get past the boys' sleeping huts before they can steal the oxen or calves. They are a polygamous society — this is indicated by the second wife's quarters, other wives' quarters, and the bride sitting place. Conversation and social interaction are of primary importance to the life of the kraal — the meeting place is central to the compound. Alcohol is a highly valued commodity — the brewery is closer to the Kraal Head's sleeping quarters than the first wife's sleeping quarters.

Everything we build—from our individual house to large cities — contains a "body language" that tells us about our beliefs, values, and mythologies. And because beliefs, values, and mythologies also shape social relationships, the environments we create will reinforce these patterns of social relationships (see Figure 5.2).

Chiefly kraal of the Ambo people. (From Hiller and Hanson, The Social Logic of Space)

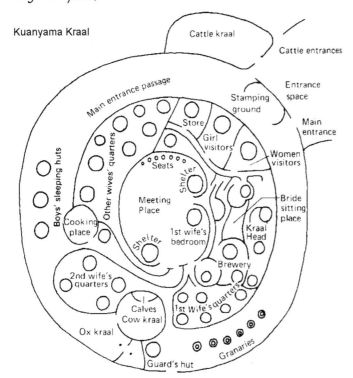

The women and children in the kraal compound do not need to get up every morning and ask themselves, "What is my place in this society?" It is written for them in the placement of walls, rooms, doorways, furniture, and every piece of mud that makes up their compound.

The arrangement of space is more than just an "indicator" or "artifact" of social relationships and thinking patterns. It is an "incarnation" of those relationships and thought forms. Incarnation is a theological word meaning "God made flesh." It carries the notion of an invisible spirit taking on a bodily form in order to communicate and make visible its essential nature. Similarly, societies can only exist as they take on a physical and material form in the spatial realm. A built environment is not just an artifact of a society. It is the "body" of that society which facilitates both internal and external relationships.

It is unlikely that the Ambo people sit down and consciously think through what arrangement of space would best reflect the social relationships within the tribe and their belief systems. It is rather an organic and unconscious process guided by the culture of that tribe which will include deep-seated beliefs about the roles of particular groups.

Similarly, the way we treat our streets is no accident. It reflects aspects of our deepest values, beliefs, and mythologies. Earlier I mentioned how our society adopted scientific thinking which sees everything in machine terms. I argued that this has led us to seeing childhood as a training ground for productive adulthood and old age as the retirement of a worn-out machine. It is therefore not just some quirk of history that has resulted in us building segregated play areas for children and retirement villages for the elderly and handing over of streets to "productive adults" in cars. If as a society we have cut ourselves off from the Child that lives in our emotional memories, then this will manifest itself in the way space is arranged. Segregated and specialised areas will be created for children's play. Play and the activity of children will not be integrated into adult space and therefore child's play will not intersect with the "serious" activities of the adult world. If we value knowledge more than wisdom or production more than reflection, then

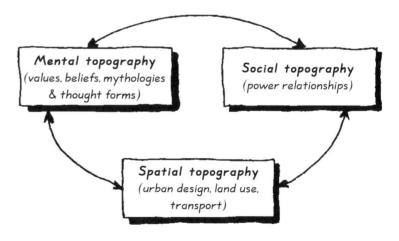

Fig. 5.2. The symbiotic relationship which forms a society and its culture.

Compare this granite seat in a Sydney mall with the loose chairs shown on p.106? What can you learn about the values of those who designed this seat (and the store owners) by looking at the physical design of the seat?

the elderly no longer have a function in society. The arrangement of space reflects our deepest values about childhood and old age.

It is therefore not enough to think that simply changing things in the physical domain will cause an automatic change in behavior. This is not to say that changes in the physical domain cannot promote deeper social and cultural change. They do. But only if they tap into, and are connected to, a set of values that lies dormant or suppressed in the collective psyche. If they don't do that, the changes in the physical domain will be subverted by the dominant values. However, what one can say with confidence is that a change in values will always result in changed spatial arrangements. That is why traffic reduction and street reclaiming promotes and celebrates a range of traditional urban values that have been eroded by the machine age.

Social/cultural change is the key

Traffic reduction, the Traffic Reduction Treaty, and street reclaiming all rely largely on breaking into the negative transport cycles at the social/cultural level rather than at the hardware level. Intervention at the social/cultural level provides a platform for the introduction of hardware solutions which reinforce social/cultural changes. But the social/cultural changes are fundamental.

Myth 3: Major Changes in Behavior Will Take Generations

At first sight the above analysis — that our physical environment is determined by our deepest beliefs and values — makes reclaiming our streets seem like a very difficult, if not impossible task. We must battle deeply ingrained values, beliefs, and mythologies, many of which lie buried deep in our psyche. This leads to a pessimistic view that significant cultural change will take generations. However, this pessimistic view is built on a faulty set of assumptions about how cultural change actually takes place.

Imagine for a moment that in eight years time, there will have been a massive change in society's attitude to the car. Just as smokers currently feel like "social lepers" — huddling in back alleys or asking permission to light up — motorists will feel antisocial when driving through public space. They will wind their window down to ask pedestrians permission to drive in their street. Imagine that this cultural revolution is so radical that people actually place digital displays in the back window of their car which flash to the world the reason this particular trip is absolutely essential. Imagine that in addition all cars must carry health warnings. Impossible? Well, so was the anti-smoking revolution eight years before it happened. So was the trash recycling revolution.

How would such a change in car culture happen? Unless we understand how cultural revolutions happen, we will stagger blind trying to change car culture.

Why rational argument does not produce cultural change

Currently, most educators, policy makers, planners, and community activists assume that cultural change happens as a result of information dissemination and "logical" argument. These people and groups working for cultural change put great faith in "getting the message out." They quote the latest research on the impacts of various pollutants on human health. They argue about safe levels and particle sizes. They seize on the latest research. Implicit in their planning or campaigning is the assumption that if they can only get someone to view the facts, they will have won one more convert. This view also assumes that you win one convert at a time and that when 51% of the population are converted, the desired social/cultural change will happen. This often leads to a pessimistic view: at the rate of current conversion, it will take decades or even a couple of generations before the change happens. I call this the "rational/linear model" of cultural change: it posits that cultural change is won through logical argument and by winning one convert at a time.

But the belief that cultural change is linear and rationally driven is a myth.

Humans do not act out of their rational brain. A number of years ago a crane was lifting a concrete block onto an inner city building site when the cable broke, sending the block hurtling onto the sidewalk and squashing two pedestrians. For days this accident occupied the news headlines. Within 24 hours there was an emergency sitting of parliament and an enquiry commissioned. The ramifications went on for months. On the same day there were two pedestrians squashed by a car. And the following day. And the day after. But there were no headlines, no calling of parliament, no enquiry. If humans were truly objective and rational, we should have reacted much more strongly to the plight of the pedestrians squashed by the cars than that of the pedestrians hit by the concrete block.

There is mounting evidence in a range of disciplines that humans do not act out of their rational brain, but out of their emotions (see Daniel Goleman, *Vital Lies, Simple Truths* and *Emotional Intelligence*). Thus we react to the story of the concrete block because secretly we all harbor a fear that while walking under a building site, the load on the crane may slip and squash us. On the other side of the ledger, we have a love affair with the car. When we are in love with someone, we are prepared to tell ourselves lies about the other person in order to preserve the "good feelings." In our heart of hearts we may know that the person we adore is a liar, or an alcoholic. But to confront the truth carries consequences we are not prepared to face. According to Goleman, our brains are physically wired in a way that allows us to filter out these unwanted "realities." As for the individual, so for society. In *Vital Lies, Simple Truths*, Coleman says that "people in groups also learn together how *not* to see — how aspects of shared experience can be veiled by self-deceits held in common .... The motivating force behind the forming of shared illusions in a group is identical to that in the self: to minimize anxiety" (p.158,& 162.) The response to the stories about the concrete block and the car are therefore not rationally driven, but driven by our emotions.

How cultural change is triggered

We must start by acknowledging that cultural revolutions do happen — as evidenced by trash recycling and smoking. However, any fair historical analysis suggests that the lead-up to a cultural revolution is not linear. One day they seem impossible, the next they happen. They are triggered by something. I use the word "triggered" because it suggests that a small movement in one direction causes a larger event to explode into existence. An additional observation is that what triggers these cultural revolutions does not seem to be obvious.

To understand what is happening in a cultural revolution, think of someone you know who has had the following experience. (We have all had this experience, but it makes it less painful to think of it having happened to someone else.)

As is the case in the family and other groups, when some aspects of the shared reality are troubling, a semblance of cozy calm can be maintained by an unspoken agreement to deny the pertinent facts.

Daniel Goleman, *Vital Lies, Simply Truths*

During the 40 days of the Gulf War that were actually violent, Americans lost 146 men and women on the battlefield. During the same 40 days, Americans lost 4,900 men and women to violence — not on the battlefield but on their own highways, in their own country.

Stanley I. Hart and Alvin L. Spivak, *Automobile Dependence and Denial*

One day you meet a friend — let's call him Bob — who has fallen madly in love with Helen. Bob can't stop raving about the wonderful qualities of Helen. She is kind, generous, and attentive. She even does voluntary work for an organization and is passionate about the cause and dedicated. You meet Bob again a week later and he has done a 360 degree turn-around. Helen-the-saint has become Helen-the-devil. Instead of being kind and generous, she is now mean and stingy. Instead of being passionate and dedicated to the cause, she is one-eyed, pig-headed, and inattentive to others. What has happened?

Our good qualities have an equal and opposite down side. Generosity is a wonderful quality. But by giving to someone we may help perpetuate a problem they have — for example, by lending a friend money every time they ask we may stop them from confronting their inability to handle finances. My ability to focus on a task is a strength. But it is also a weakness when I am so focused I forget to pay bills, to stay in contact with my friends, or to talk to my kids. When we fall in love with someone, at a subconscious level we choose to see the good side of this person's qualities and filter out the negative side of these same qualities — just as we choose to embrace the positives of the car and to filter out the negatives. However, in human

Our mental landscape is not a simple, black-and-white world. It contains paradoxical values that stand opposed to each other. Cultural revolutions happen when we renegotiate the relationship between paradoxical values.

relationships, something often happens which causes a flip at the subconscious level. Maybe the partner comes home late or forgets a birthday or burns the dinner. This small event becomes the trigger for a realignment in the filters. The other person may not have changed one iota, but the way the brain processes the incoming data has. The brain looks at exactly the same quality and embraces the negative side of the quality while filtering out the positive.

The same process happens in cultural life. Take the car, for example. We have already noted the incredible paradoxical nature of the car. It is both a blessing and a curse. It facilitates planned exchanges but destroys our home territory and our spontaneous exchanges. When in the car, we highly value speed. When out of the car, the same speed becomes a curse. Our mental landscape is not a simple, black-and-white world. It contains paradoxical values that stand opposed to each other. For example, in the illustration I gave above as to why we segregate children's play out of the adult world, there are a whole lot of other values in our mental landscape that stand paradoxically opposed to this segregation. Parents wish they did not have to chauffeur their children everywhere; we see great value in having children develop good citizenship skills; watching children play does bring us some pleasure. How are we as a society to handle the incredible tension between these paradoxical values? We use the same strategy employed by individuals: we create a simplified world by choosing subconsciously to filter out one side of the paradox.

But out of sight is not out of mind. The tension is simply moved underground rather than being dealt with on the surface. Small events (equivalent to the partner burning dinner) will add extra weight to one side of the tension, causing a rupture and realignment. Thus, cultural change is triggered subconsciously — much as an earthquake is triggered: subterranean conflicting planes of values and experience-based emotions move over each other creating increasing tension which must be resolved when the tension is great enough.

There is another dimension to this story. The paradoxical values are not just inside our heads. They are also outside. Different groups in society have resolved their internal dilemmas in different ways. So if there are competing voices in both our internal and external world, which values and beliefs do we build into the fabric of the city around us? As in any marriage, the competing voices have a particular kind of relationship to each other, and it is the shape of this relationship that gets built into the urban form. For example, currently the voice that values speed has the upper hand over the voice that values safety and amenity. Therefore we construct streets that facilitate speed rather than a vibrant community life. This does not mean that we do not value safety, amenity, and community life. It is just that we have allowed these values to be dominated and pushed down by the voice that demands speed.

Cultural revolutions are triggered when we renegotiate the relationship between paradoxical voices. Therefore, far from being a difficult task, triggering a cultural revolution only requires identifying existing values that are being "bullied into submission" by their opposite and giving the subjugated value a voice. The most powerful way to do this is not to attack the dominant voice but to celebrate that which is pushed down.

Once the mental landscape has been changed (a change in the way the paradoxical voices relate), the physical landscape will look after itself. For example, if people take back their streets in their head and create a better balance between their desires for speed and their desires for safety, community, and a quality urban environment, they will automatically drive less and drive slower. They will demand that governments change policies that favor speed over amenity. They will walk, cycle, and use public transport more and demand these options will be given greater public support.

People of all ages — like this New York woman — like to dress up and join in celebrations. Celebrating the potential of our streets may help trigger significant changes in car culture.

The power of celebration

The trigger for some cultural revolutions is a "new experience of place." Cultural revolutions often take place within the envelope of a celebration and new cultural experiences. For example, prior to 1988 in Brisbane we had no outdoor dining at restaurants (in spite of our subtropical climate). We had no "higher-density" inner-city living. However, World Expo 88 is credited with changing all that and with triggering a demand for a greater range of restaurants, sidewalk dining, and cosmopolitan, inner-city living. The demand for change was not created by dissemination of new information but by a new experience of place that changed perceptions of how other spaces could be experienced.

In celebrations we get good feelings from "letting our hair down" and bonding with those around us. These positive emotional experiences become attached to the thing we are celebrating or to the venue of the celebration. The celebration is therefore a powerful way of adding emotional weight to something that may trigger a much larger change in cultural outlook. For example, a celebration of a particular river may trigger a change in cultural attitude to water pollution in general. This is why I believe celebrating the potential role of streets by drawing on a rich tradition is so important in triggering cultural change towards the car.

Pulling the trigger

The above analysis leads to three propositions about how someone working for cultural change can "pull the trigger."

- Cultural change (individual or collective) can be triggered by boosting existing values which stand paradoxically opposed to those holding most power in the existing culture. The change in power relationships triggers the brokering of a "new deal" which becomes the new culture.
- Cultural change is more likely to be triggered through boosting the "marginalized values" rather than by trying to denigrate the values that currently hold the dominant power.
- Factual information is important in cultural change, but as a "post-hoc rationalization;" that is, the individual or society must be able to justify the reasons for embracing the new position.

Here I give away some of the trade secrets of the *Traffic Reduction Kit* process. Instead of tackling the negatives of the car head on, it deliberately amplifies and legitimizes the suppressed voice — the voice that says "I am sick and tired of the way traffic is eroding my quality of life." The use of Treaty Advocates to share the video with their neighbors and the Street Party are ways of giving people an experience of what their street may be like and strengthening an internal voice that says "I want a street rich in social and cultural diversity." The term "street reclaiming" is chosen to give legitimacy to this suppressed voice. In addition, the material in this book and the educational material in the Kit make conscious an internal values di-

Cultural change can be triggered by tapping existing values — such as the need for children to have independent mobility.

lemma of speed versus amenity. Up until now, people have been able to externalize this dilemma — me as resident versus them as motorists. Instead, this material internalizes the dilemma — me as resident versus me as motorist. This establishes an internal dialogue between the paradoxically opposed voices of motorist and resident. In the dialogue, participants are forced to broker a peace deal between the two parties. For some, this deal may mean ditching their car altogether. For others, it will mean that they will minimize their car use and act as guests when driving through other people's neighborhoods. It is the brokering of this new deal which is the stuff of cultural revolutions.

Now if I am reading the cultural landscape right, we are currently experiencing a fairly major cultural revolution where large portions of the population are once again embracing "urbanity" as a positive quality. The "coffee shop revolution" in Canada, Australia, and the USA is just one indicator of this cultural shift, as is the dramatic movement of professionals away from the quarter-acre block to inner-city apartments. This desire for urban amenity is fueling an anti-traffic sentiment which has become the number one political issue in many cities. If tapped correctly, this cultural revolution could trigger an even larger cultural revolution — a major change in car culture.

MYTH BUSTER *Car culture can be changed quickly*

Traffic reduction and street reclaiming do not accept that major cultural change will take generations or that it will happen through the mounting of logical argument. They are built on the notion that car culture can be changed quickly by celebrating the traditional urban values that are being subjugated by car culture.

Myth 4: Streets and Cities Can Be Treated as a "Machine"

The planning and engineering professions are built on a "machine model" of the city. In other words, there is an assumption that streets, and the city as a whole, operates as a giant machine. It is assumed that by changing the physical design of the various parts of this machine we can make it function more efficiently. It is therefore no accident that streets are viewed as a machine for moving traffic. The job of the engineer is to optimize the efficiency of this machine: making intersections more efficient, coordinating traffic lights, identifying and removing conflict points, etc. If we use a machine model of streets, it makes a lot of sense to do these things.

Efficient machines have a number of qualities:

- Every part of a machine has a clearly defined and specialized function.
- Ambiguity and spontaneity undermine the efficiency of a machine. There can be no room for "randomness" or "creativity" in a machine. Efficiency depends on total ordering.

However, the machine mode is an entirely inappropriate model for the city. It is true that aspects of a city act like a machine — just as the heart in the human body acts like a pump or arms act as complex levers. However, it is not possible to understand a friend or your lover by understanding how their "mechanical bits" work. It cannot explain why, when you first met your lover, the rate at which their heart pumped blood increased. Your friend or lover is a complex web of mental, emotional, spiritual, and physical realities. I have argued that cities are also complex webs of social, cultural, and physical realities. Scientific and mechanistic thinking has its place in the city: for designing sewerage systems, increasing the carrying capacity of roads, or designing chairs that do not collapse. However, such a thinking framework must be subservient to a more holistic model.

A more appropriate model for understanding cities and designing solutions is an "ecosystem model." An ecosystem model recognizes that the complex web of relationships in a city involves more than just the physical elements that can be touched and smelt. And it recognizes that all elements are in a dynamic and largely unpredictable relationship. For example, very small changes in the social dimension

In practice, the planning of cities merges almost imperceptibly into the problems of cities, and those into the economics and sociology and politics of cities, and those in turn into the entire socio-economic-political-cultural life of the time; there is no end, no boundary, to the relationships....

Peter Hall, *Cities of Tomorrow*

can produce large chain reactions that will radically change the physical environment.

The ecosystem model requires streets and the city to be treated in a way that is exactly opposite to that demanded by the machine model:

• The more "functions" being performed by a space, the greater the efficiency of that space as a mechanism for facilitating exchanges

• Randomness, ambiguity, and contradiction improve the efficiency of an ecosystem as a mechanism for exchange.

Let me explain further. Christopher Alexander argues that city environments should be treated as poetry rather than as prose. Prose is machine-like, with a logical, precise, predetermined, single meaning. In contrast, poetry is organic, does not follow the rules of logic, and does not have a precise, predetermined, single meaning. Poetry layers meanings, often combining contradictory elements. In prose, the writer intends the reader to "understand" something. In poetry, the writer wants the reader to "feel"' something. In prose, what is to be understood is predetermined by the author. In poetry, the writer gives readers the freedom to experience their own emotions and to resolve the tensions created by ambiguity and contradiction in their own way.

Spaces treated as poetry rather than as prose do not impose a single, rational function. For example, a street cannot be given the singular function of "moving cars". Contradictory functions are encouraged and strengthened. Meanings and functions are layered into the space. This layering of meanings in space is not a process of simple addition but a process of multiplication. Each new meaning which is added enriches all those meanings which already exist. Such layering of functions and meanings therefore makes a space inherently more efficient and gives the users of the space a richer experience.

In poetry, the poet does not try and explain the contradictions or ambiguity. In fact, it is the ambiguity, the self-contradiction, which gives poetry its depth of meaning and its ability to rouse the senses. Poetry is a form of chaos with structure or structured chaos. I postulate that if we researched what imparts to one space a stronger sense of placeness than to another, we would find that this is determined, in large part, by the degree to which meanings and functions have been layered and the degree of ambiguity and contradiction in the design. The reason such spaces are inherently

We are learning in other areas, such as natural ecology, health, and even education, that understanding anything less than a whole habitat, a whole being, or a whole system is likely to be ineffective and sometimes harmful, especially over the long term. What whole in a society, we must ask, deserves understanding as an organic unity more than the city?

Kenneth Schneider, *On the Nature of Cities*

A space does not become a place until it used for purposes not intended by the designer. The ambiguity inherent in most art allows it to be used as a play-thing for children... and adults.

more attractive to us is that they appeal to the storyteller and playful child in our head: the space provides us with props with which we can create a wide variety of "realities." We can return day after day and create new stories. Such spaces stimulate the senses and force us to be creative by inventing our own "grand scheme" or "plot-framework" to impart meaning to the space. Spaces treated as prose are over-designed, containing a plot-framework which is created in the mind of the designer and imposed on all other users of the space. As such, they do not have the power to evoke the storyteller in our head or to stir our senses. The story has already been told.

Seeing streets as a machine for moving vehicles is to impose a very narrow plot-framework. As I have shown above, streets also serve social and cultural functions. Maximizing their efficiency to move vehicles may undermine the social and cultural life of the city to the extent of jeopardizing the whole viability of the city as a social and cultural organism. In his celebrated book *City of Quartz*, Mike Davis foreshadowed the Los Angeles riots seeing them as a result of the segregation created by the design of the city. Ironically, treating streets as machines to maximize movement of vehicles can actually undermine the whole efficiency of the city as a mechanism for facilitating diverse exchanges — and it may even undermine the entire economic viability of the city.

City character is blurred until every place becomes more like every other place, all adding up to Noplace.

Jane Jacobs, *The Death and Life of Great American Cities*

Only when the mechanical energies of the Engineer are brought into line with all other aspects of the city, and these reunited in the services for life, can he change from blundering giant into helpful Hercules.

Patrick Geddes (1917)

The design of this street and the design of the shade structures allow for multiple functions.

There is another powerful reason for allowing ambiguity in city design. At different stages of our development and different seasons of our life we need different types of "archetypical places." As children we need a variety of places: secret places, places where we can practice place making, places to develop citizenship skills, places to take risks, places to develop physical coordination. As adults we also need a variety of places: places that connect us back to our childhood; places to people-watch; in times of grief, places of solitude and the soothing sound of water; and in our old age, places to ponder and share our wisdom. Even at the same stage of life, different people need different kinds of archetypical places. All of these archetypical places need certain elements to make them work. The richest places are those that have the flexibility to be used as a wide range of archetypical places. That means leaving enough ambiguity so that the users of the space can adapt it to their particular needs at that moment of time. Neighborhoods that do not have the flexability to fulfil the full range of archetypical places cannot meet all the social, spiritual, emotional, cultural, and physical needs of the residents. The livability of any neighborhood is dependent on the accessibility of these archetypical places with their layered meanings and high degree of ambiguity and contradiction.

 MYTH BUSTER *Streets are not machines, but complex ecosystems*

Traffic reduction and street reclaiming deliberately seek to layer multiple functions into street space and to increase opportunity for spontaneous exchanges. They treat the street as a complex ecosystem rather than as a simplistic, mono-dimensional machine and see ambiguity and randomness as central to efficiency.

Myth 5: Human Nature is Basically Selfish

As mentioned above, authorities have been besotted with hardware solutions to problems like traffic. They have ignored "social capital" as a means of solving problems. The reason for this is that authorities proceed on the assumption that human nature is basically selfish and that the government's role is to control and regulate this selfishness. Sure, there is some appeal to human goodness, but this is not the basis on which policy is constructed. The rule is competition. The exception is cooperation.

One of the great paradoxes of humans is that we are both selfish and generous. To a large extent, the balance we strike between these two is environmentally determined. If we are in a mean environment, we will tend to act mean. If we are in an environment of goodwill, we will tend to be more giving.

I am convinced that social problems must be solved first and foremost through trading on social capital. Any hardware solutions must have as their primary basis both an investment in social capital and a trading on this capital. The processes outlined in this book for tackling traffic problems are just one example of how this can be done.

The three untapped resources that make up social capital are altruism, creative wealth, and resourcefulness.

Altruism

Some years back Chris Cunningham introduced me to the idea of the "altruistic surplus" of cities. Being altruistic means performing a task to benefit another with no payback. Earlier I called the altruistic surplus "goodwill infrastructure." Chris Cunningham argues that what makes one city more livable than another is not its economic surplus but what the citizens are willing to put into the collective enterprise above and beyond what they draw out. I was attracted to this idea because it addresses something that had always puzzled me. As someone who has had the privilege of visiting many cities around the world, I am always struck by the feeling one gets when first arriving in a city. Some cities feel welcoming, safe, and nurturing. Others feel mean and dangerous. When I thought back to my experiences in these cities, it was the altruistic surplus that made the difference.

Portland, Oregon, is held up as one of the great livable cities of the world. In Portland I was struck with the high level of citizen involvement in building a quality urban environment. For example, there is a people's square in the middle of Portland, which was once a car park. This huge public square was built through individual donations. There are thousands of paving bricks in the square which bear the names of residents who donated money towards the square. The family I stayed with were

If competition and conflict were really the ruling forces in society, then our cities would resemble Beirut or Sarajevo. If cities are working even tolerably well — and most of them work surprisingly well — then it must be because considerable numbers of citizens are contributing more than they are drawing out. The trait of altruism, subject of the greatest suspicion by most economic philosophers, is the distinguishing force that keeps cities functioning more or less well. We take it for granted in every aspect of our lives.

Chris Cunningham, *Towards a New Planning Framework*

We are yet to discover how the altruism, creativity, and resourcefulness of citizens can be deliberately tapped as a way of solving problems and making our cities better places to live.

Here two people with disabilities take a child on an urban outing.

What makes one city more "civilized" than another is the extent of altruistic activities.

helping to raise $600,000 to buy a piece of bushland on a mountain to preserve for future generations. All my enduring memories of great cities have their genesis in this spirit of altruism: two young people pushing an elderly blind man in a wheel chair in a bike lane in Groningen; the lady in Hamburg who did not just give me directions to the youth hostel, but walked me there and along the way gave me a guided tour of the city.

Cognitive psychologists tell us some interesting things about altruism — it feeds on itself. If you create an environment in which it is the norm to give to others without expecting a payback, then the levels of altruism rise. Unlike money, the more you spend the altruistic surplus, the more you have to spend. The great thing about tapping altruism as a way of solving problems like traffic is that it not only helps get the problem solved, it also increases the size of the altruistic surplus which can then be tapped to help solve other problems.

Chris Cunningham argues that monetary wealth has a tendency to diminish the altruistic surplus. It is in times of need that altruism is drawn forth. In the West we have reached a high degree of personal comfort and there is a large emphasis on the individual pursuit of happiness. If altruism is the civilizing force of a city and this altruism is not currently being solicited through exposure to need, then the political body must find other catalysts if we are to build the altruistic surplus as our most valuable commodity. I believe that trading on the altruistic surplus to help solve the city's most pressing social and cultural problems is one way of building this altruism.

I have been constantly amazed in the initial trials of the *Traffic Reduction Kit* at how people do respond if you unashamedly appeal to their altruism. I find a great deal of skepticism among decision-makers that people will act altruistically for the good of the city. There is an underlying assumption that greed and self-interest are the only things that motivate people. Unfortunately, proceeding to plan on the basis of this assumption produces the very qualities that are presumed to dominate people in the first place.

Creative wealth

Humans are remarkably creative. Currently, governments are loath to unleash this creative power in solving problems. Instead they commission consultants or undertake studies which simply rehash the same old "solutions." A number of years ago I ran the community consultation program for a major urban renewal project in Brisbane. One of the issues we had to deal with was "mixed use" — the idea of creating a greater variety of exchange opportunities close to home. So we ran an ideas competition, inviting residents, children, and professional planners to submit ideas for how spaces in the urban renewal area could be converted to mixed use. The range of ideas was astonishing, including ways that community or commercial facilities could be built right in the centre of some streets while still keeping lane widths equal to existing lanes in the area. Some of these ideas were the genesis of the idea of street reclaiming.

To tap the creative wealth of a city, we must establish processes that allow new ideas to be developed and tried out at the local level. This means handing responsibility for problems back to the community and allowing them to evolve their own solutions. They certainly will not come up with creative solutions while some government department accepts responsibility and pretends that it has the solutions or will find them given a little more time.

To make this responsibility stick and to get people working together on creative solutions, the process must work with an identifiable community. In the case of the *Traffic Reduction Treaty* process I decided to work with neighborhoods at the single street level for three reasons. Firstly, this is where most traffic is generated. Secondly, it is one of the smallest community units — smaller than, say, a school, shopping precinct, or large employer. Thirdly, there is a lot of emotion attached already to the way traffic has impacted on the cohesion of a street community. This does not mean that other processes cannot be developed that target different community groupings (Appendix 1 outlines a traffic reduction process I tried out with a school where we were dealing with safety issues). My point is that in order to get people working on finding creative solutions, government can not simply issue a press release saying, "It is time the public owned their part of the traffic problem and did something about it." The responsibility has to be handed to an identifiable group of citizens who already act as a community of interest.

Resourcefulness

Resourcefulness is the ability to "make do" with the material and tools at hand. It is an expression of human creativity, but applied to the way resources get used. It is a way of taking "junk" and giving it new value. It is the ability to stretch limited resources. For example, in the first trial of the *Traffic Reduction Kit* in Brisbane, the neighborhood decided to create planter boxes out of concrete pipe off-cuts that one of the residents had access to. Thus waste would be recycled into a product with value.

It makes eminent sense to challenge the community to trade on its resourcefulness in solving problems. For example, asking residents to do their own street reclaiming will save larger cities millions of dollars in traditional traffic calming costs — even if the city makes some contribution to material costs. The great benefits of this go beyond dollar savings, however. Calling on people's resourcefulness results in products which are more powerfully stamped with the unique personality and character of those doing the creating than a ready-made solution bought with buckets of money. It is this unique signature which gives residents a much stronger sense of place and belonging. It is also this signature which is needed to convey the message to motorists that they are in someone's "private space" — a space that is highly valued and loved.

 MYTH BUSTER *Tapping social capital is a key to evolving solutions*

The *Traffic Reduction Treaty* and street reclaiming are built on a blatant appeal to people's altruism, creative wealth, and resourcefulness. The building of this social capital is not only important for the ongoing evolution of traffic reduction solutions, but for the evolution of solutions to a wide range of other urban problems. This social capital is also what makes cities and neighborhoods life-enhancing.

Myth 6: Economics Can Be Divorced from Everyday Life

In our modern society, "the economy" is spoken of and treated as if it had a life of its own. To most of us, the economy is shrouded in mystery. Only economists, politicians, and the initiated appear to be able to penetrate its sacred veil.

Politicians often announce that major projects, like new mines or highways, will be "good for the economy." But what on earth is "the economy?" And how does "the economy" relate to urban design and transportation? In the first chapter of this book, I argued that cities were an invention to maximize the diversity of exchange opportunities while minimizing the cost of accessing those exchanges. Cities were an invention to improve the economy with which exchanges could be made. The whole city is therefore "an economy of exchange." By losing sight of the original intention of cities and by turning the economy into a world in its own right, we have made a number of fundamental errors in how we approach both the economy and the design of our cities.

Focusing on the wrong goal

What is the ultimate goal of an economy? It is certainly not to simply produce ever increasing GDP (Gross Domestic Product) figures. It surely must be to increase the utility that citizens derive from being part of a collective enterprise. Utility is not the same thing as consumer goods or money in the bank. Utility is the ability for some commodity or social arrangement to enhance our quality of life. A consumer good has no utility unless it enhances our life in some way. The exercise machine gathering dust in the attic may have added to the GDP, but it is not adding one ounce of value to the quality of our life.

The other day I walked past a bakery with a friend who is an astute business woman. Behind the counter was a young girl with a smile that oozed warmth and welcome. My friend commented that the smile was worth a million dollars. Now the bread from this bakery may cost the same as bread from other bakeries. But you get more than bread at this shop. You get a smile that lifts your spirits. The good feeling you get from this young girl's smile is "utility." It is intimately bound to an economic exchange, but there is a value in that smile that cannot be measured in the GDP.

Take another example. You go to a concert to listen to your favorite artists. They sing and play a new song that was inspired by a conversation they had on the streets the week before. The ticket to the concert was the same price as last time you went, but

We can't have a sustainable economy unless we build a physical setting to house it. The physical setting we presently dwell in itself exhausts our capital....

There are some things we can predict about the physical arrangement of life in the coming decades. The most obvious is that we will have to rebuild our towns and cities in order to have any kind of advanced economy at all. In fact, this enterprise may turn out to be the engine that powers our economy for years to come, much the same way that the suburban build-out did...

James Howard Kunstler, *The Geography of Nowhere*

A sustainable strategy devised for urban systems is based on raising complexity; or put another way, on increasing the probability of contact between the different elements without any increase in consumption of energy and resources.

Salvador Rueda et al., *The Sustainable City*

There is something about cities that increases the propensity and capacity of people to create value for each other ... If everyone's thoughts were the same as your thoughts, you might as well just converse with yourself. More important for our purposes, variation among people is a source (maybe even the source) of value creation .... value creation, which can also be called cultural evolution.

Mike Greenberg, *The Poetics of Cities*

the experience was richer this time. The conversation the artists had on the street inspired them to add utility or value to the concert.

And this is what the city is all about: value-adding to utility. Each exchange carries the potential to enrich other exchanges without increasing the cost of transacting that exchange.

However, utility is not just related to the quantity or quality of material goods. Mike Greenberg explains:

> It might also mean shorter or more pleasant commutes to work or shopping; cleaner, safer, more beautiful, and more diverting parks; better schools and more fully stocked libraries; more enjoyable music on the radio and more interesting exhibits at the museum; more opportunities to make new friends and keep old ones. Even in the mundane world of commodity exchange, "better off" entails more than purely quantitative improvements. It can involve intangible emotional, sensual, and intellectual rewards — the unexpected pleasure of the Indian restaurant that didn't exist last year ... (*The Poetics of Cities*, p.47.)

Economic strategies for cities must carry the same goal as transport and urban design strategies: increasing the efficiency with which diverse exchanges

Economic exchanges are part of a total social/cultural experience: in this case, the bike ride to the coffee shop, interaction with the waiter and other patrons and some people-watching. Destroy any one of these elements and you may destroy the entire economic exchange.

can be transacted while at the same time increasing the utility inherent in those exchanges. The economy is not therefore some external reality. It is intimately bound into the totality of our life. It certainly is not just the exchanging of money for goods and services. The "economy of exchange," facilitated by the city, is an old person on a seat supervising neighborhood children playing in the street. It is the listening ear offered by the butcher. It is the street busker. It is the eccentric on the milk crate playing a tin whistle. It is the increased variety of restaurants in our district. It is the surprise find at the second-hand shop. It is a sense of home we get each time we pass the tree where we stole our first kiss. It is the sense of belonging we get from helping someone who has fallen down. It is the stranger who tells us tales of exotic places. It is the street wisdom we gather from our elders. The health of an economy must be measured by how well it is facilitating these diverse, life-enhancing exchanges.

The whole city is the marketplace

Mike Greenberg contends:

> Noneconomic exchange is as important to the creation of value as economic exchange; such noneconomic places as parks and sidewalks are as essential to the marketplace as shops and offices and factories. While "the economy" of the

The bottom line was this: When the car industry commenced its long, slow death — still in progress — and the economy of Detroit failed, the community failed with it. For the situation in a big city is the same as in a small town: the economy is the community. Without one, you cannot have the other.

James Howard Kunstler, *The Geography of Nowhere*

Eating of this icecream is part of a total social/cultural experience made all the more pleasurable by the balloon busker. The balloon busker is probably aiding the icecream shop to sell more icecreams, and the icecream shop is probably helping the busker earn a living.

The neighborhood is potentially the most efficient nexus of social, cultural, and economic exchange.

Mike Greenberg, *The Poetics of Cities*

economists inhabits an abstract number-space, the economy of the real world happens in physical space, in the places where you and I and our neighbors interact (*The Poetics of Cities*, p.53.)

Business people are yet to realize that the whole city is essential to the well-being of their enterprise. The effectiveness with which their business can operate is dependent on the efficiency of the city as an mechanism for exchange. Astute business people know that the best form of advertising is "word of mouth." But how do these verbal exchanges take place? In the traditional city, largely in the streets and squares. A vibrant spontaneous exchange realm in the city is therefore crucial for generating new business. While the spontaneous realm does not enter the calculations of the economist, it is one of the primary generators of new business in the city.

Drawing a distinction between costs and benefits

The next major problem with the way "the economy" is viewed by economists and politicians is that there is no way of discerning what adds utility and value and what undermines utility and value. This means that wars are good for "the economy" because they improve the GDP. So are cars and freeways. So is burning fossil fuels. But clearly some things add utility and others don't.

James Kunstler in *The Geography of Nowhere* discusses the "boom years" when American cities spread out into the countryside:

The distinction between the booming economy and what that boom yielded can't be stressed enough. The great suburban build-out generated huge volumes of business. The farther apart things spread, the more cars were needed to link up the separate things, the more asphalt and cement were needed for roads, bridges and parking lots, the more copper for electric cables, et cetera. Each home needed its own washing machine... In a culture with no other values, this could easily be construed as a good thing. Indeed, the relentless expansion of consumer goodies became increasingly identified with our national character as the American Way of Life. Yet not everyone failed to notice that the end product of all this furious commerce-for-its-own-sake was a trashy and preposterous human habitat with no future (p.107-8.)

While we may argue about whether or not cars and freeways add utility (I would argue that they do until they reach a certain critical density), one important distinction has to be made: they are a *means* to utility rather than utility in their own right. They are therefore a *facilitatory cost* we pay to get access to exchange opportunities. It thus seems to be extreme folly to confuse costs with benefits and to count these facilitatory costs as an indicator of a healthy economy. The goal of any city is to reduce these costs in order to increase the economy of exchange. Even if we reduce exchange to a narrow definition of exchange of goods for money, transport is still a facilitatory cost that undermines efficiency.

 A healthy economy equals exchange efficiency

Traffic reduction and street reclaiming are built on a holistic notion of a healthy economy which involves
- minimizing the of costs of facilitating exchanges
- increasing the diversity of exchange opportunities in order to feed the creative life of the city and to add value to all exchanges
- increasing the multiplier effect of money in the economy by reducing the amount being spent on burning fuel and increasing the amount being spent on the labour content of products and services.

Myth 7: It Is Important to Get the Big Picture Right First

Planning professionals, and the general public, have been besotted with "getting the big picture right." We expend enormous amounts of money on master planning: transport master plans, land-use master plans, cultural master plans, integrated master plans, and regional master plans. When things are going wrong we are fond of saying, "there was not enough planning" — by which we mean big-picture planning. Now while a certain amount of master planning is necessary, I believe we have the balance entirely wrong.

This traditional approach is based in the machine model — it is very easy to master-plan a machine. But cities, as we have seen, are not a machine and in fact do not respond well to being master-planned.

A useful model for understanding the role of planning in cities is to consider it as the art/science of promoting urban vitality. This involves not only the art of diagnosing what saps or destroys the life and vitality of urban environments, but also of finding ways to reverse the negative feedback loops that produce these outcomes. This requires small changes that will produce a chain reaction which enhances rather than destroys. This approach would need to understand the small details that directly promote health and vitality. For example, it may tell us about the importance of seating and water in public spaces, of buildings addressing the street to create a sense of intimacy and safety, of maximum distances between

Planning for chaotic systems may be more successful when it is viewed as a succession of judicious "nudges" rather than as a step-by-step recipe. For in chaotic systems, relatively small changes in inputs can have a dramatic effect on system behavior. This is a salutary reminder that, in planning, the details can be just as important as the broad strokes.

T. J. Cartwright, *"Planning and Chaos Theory"*

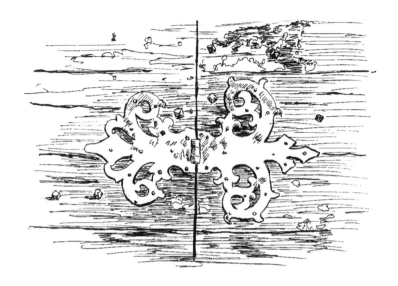

It is the small details of a city that delight and surprise. The panoramic views can be absorbed in a few minutes. It is the details that entertain and give colour to every-day life.

doorways and windows in buildings for drawing the pedestrian on, of the importance of connectivity between exchange spaces, etc.

I believe this model of promoting urban vitality has another interesting application — one which challenges the myth that if you get the big picture right, everything will fall into line below that. Organisms usually get sick by one unhealthy cell infecting another. They get better by creating healthy cells that in turn affect other cells. This seems to ring true with all that we have said about streets. One parent deciding to drive a child to school can set off a chain reaction that has an impact on the entire city. Therefore, any master plan for reforming the transport system of a city must be focused on the task of creating healthy neighborhood cells, not on trying to reform the entire system from the top down.

 Detail is the key, not the big picture

Traffic reduction and street reclaiming see community building at the neighborhood level, together with building a robust local economy, as the key to tackling the root-causes of city-wide traffic problems. Creating healthy "cells" is the key to creating a healthy "body."

Myth 8: Fixing Problems Requires Greater Levels of Intervention

We assume that fixing problems like transportation requires high levels of government intervention and control. However, the exact opposite may be the case. In other words, the problems we are currently experiencing may be caused by over-planning — in the sense of imposing order from outside. What is needed is "good" planning rather than "more" planning — "good" planning being planning which reduces the need for "control" while "more" planning creates higher levels of regulation and intervention.

Let me explain. Kid's games have rules to govern the game. In a game of hide and seek, one person must close their eyes and count to a predetermined number. The other players hide. The seeker then looks for those hiding and the first one found will become the seeker in the next round of the game. These rules create a simple structure which maximizes freedom of expression while still giving shape and purpose to the game. Every game is therefore unique although still instantly recognizable as a game of hide and seek. If the rules are expanded past an optimum point, the game will become increasingly predictable and more and more energy will be diverted from playing the game into policing the rules. The game will lose its appeal to the children. The game is therefore an interesting mix of minimized order and spontaneity or chaos.

Nature uses the same process for creating incredibly complex structures and organisms. Most organisms and cells contain a "descriptor" which contain what resembles the rules governing a game. Nature simplifies the rules contained in descriptors and basically says, "cells can go wherever they like as long as they obey these simple rules." Scientists are now starting to unravel these encoded descriptors and can even replicate the process on a computer. They can instruct the computer randomly to place a dot on the screen. They then instruct it to place another dot anywhere on the screen, provided it bears a particular mathematical relationship to the first. As this process unfolds, the first pictures that emerge look like a chaotic mess of dots. But gradually a shape will emerge, for example the shape of a fern leaf. Every time they run the experiment, they will get a fern leaf, but each will be a unique creation never to be repeated. In nature, the greater the control factor in the descriptors, the less room there is for this unique character to unfold and the less efficient the organism.

Let me relate this to urban environments. Earlier we explored a typical kraal of the Ambo people. On close examination we would find that all kraals of the Ambo people have similar structures but each carries its own unique personality and character.

Randomness emerges, in effect, as a form of necessary order both in spatial arrangements and in social systems.

Bill Hillier and Julienne Hanson, *The Social Logic of Space*

Each element is placed at random but is controlled by a hidden descriptor — the Ambo people's mental and social topography. Similarly, we could argue that prior to the advent of the modern town planning movement, it was the mental and social topography of city residents that turned randomness into order and produced cities that were legible, highly efficient in their form and aesthetically pleasing to the eye.

In *The Social Logic of Space*, Hillier and Hanson experiment with reducing particular social values into descriptors which they use to control the random placement of buildings in space. Like the fern leaf experiment, the computer generates urban forms that are typical of the urban form generated by the societies subscribing to its values.

Developing a city-wide traffic reduction program

A good city-wide traffic reduction program needs at least the following elements:

- Detailed mapping of where the inefficiencies in the existing transport system are and where maximum reductions can be achieved with minimum investment.
- Detailed mapping of the negative feedback loops which create these inefficiencies — for example, a negative school traffic loop (see p. 154.) These inefficiency loops must include physical, social, and cultural realities.
- Strategies which are aimed at reversing these inefficiency loops by tackling the links easiest to reverse.
- An overall cultural change strategy built on identifying potential triggers and programs that activate these triggers.
- A physical infrastructure plan. The introduction of hardware items such as car share clubs or public transport initiatives must be tied to the reaching of particular stages in the overall cultural change plan. In other words, these hardware items need a certain level of cultural change if they are to survive and reach their potential. A premature introduction can mean they are stillborn.
- An "economic prosperity plan" which uses traffic reduction as a catalyst for new and more efficient business (see Appendix 2.)

The implications for planning are twofold. Firstly, if we are to develop urban forms that are aesthetically pleasing and more efficient, then we must minimize the control functions. This becomes a task of taking regulations and bylaws and finding the "social logic" that lies behind them in the first place. We may find that there are a number of fundamental descriptors that cover volumes and volumes of existing regulations. For example, one descriptor that may cover dozens of existing laws and bylaws may be the following one: "This city will not allow any activity which does not encourage fuller participation in community life by those on the margin of community life. No activity will be permitted that increases the marginality of any person or group."

The second implication is that planners will have to see themselves less as manipulators of hardware items in physical space and more as dealers in values, beliefs, and mythologies. Their role should not be to impose some order in community life, but rather to facilitate a dialogue between the competing and paradoxical voices we discussed earlier. This involves helping people confront their own internal contradictions, such as the one between speed and amenity. The ensuing cultural change will automatically result in changes in the physical environment.

If our cities have become inefficient because we have moved many of the spontaneous exchanges into the planned exchange realm and because we are investing more and more of our energy in trying to "control" the city, then the answer is not more planning (read control). The solutions lie in handing back control to the grassroots.

MYTH BUSTER *Good planning means less contol*

Traffic reduction and street reclaiming have at their heart a redemocratization of our streets, a handing back of control. This will lead to much more efficient cities and neighborhoods that are stamped with their own character and personality. Such places are inherently more efficient, stimulating, and satisfying.

Some guidelines

Drawn from the material in this chapter, here are some guidelines for addressing a broad range of problems in our cities.

Software before hardware: Most problems can be solved by making changes in the social and cultural rather than the physical landscape. These "software solutions" will require some hardware items just as the recycling revolution required recycling bins, collection services, and associated industries. But the social/cultural changes rather than the hardware items are the drivers.

System-wide efficiency, not part optimization: Streets and the city must be treated as a complex ecosystem, not as a simplistic machine. Improving the efficiency of one part (for example roads for moving traffic) may damage the efficiency of the entire system.

Low tech, not high tech solutions: The one thing we know from history is that new technologies have a hidden sting in their tail, namely unforeseeable consequences. For example, the car was hailed as the great solution to the pollution caused by horses in the street. One should always ask if it is possible to solve the problem with a solution which is less high tech.

Layer functions and accept contradictions, do not rationalize: The efficiency of any ecosystem, unlike that of a machine, relies on the layering of functions and on a certain amount of ambiguity and messiness.

Eliminate existing inefficiencies before creating a new infrastructure: In management terms, it makes no sense for a factory which is experiencing a peak demand one month a year to build a new factory to accommodate this peak. They need to first look inward to see if there are existing inefficiencies that can be eliminated or whether the existing infrastructure can be used to spread the load.

Local before regional solutions: Regional solutions must be based on workable, local strategies. Traffic reduction strategies must be centred in identifiable communities of interest: for example a street, a school, the local shopping center, a major employer.

Minimize control functions: Mechanisms need to be found to reduce levels of regulation and control rather than to increase them.

chapter six

STREETS AHEAD

Dare to dream ... and create

The proclaimers of change
Pipers and drummers on stilts (and wearing hub-caps) take over a major road in Brisbane. They invite us to imagine a future different than the present.

How We Ended Up With the Worst of Both Worlds

Part of our cultural heritage in Australia, the UK, the USA, and Canada has been a strong anti-city bias. Influenced by the havoc that the industrial revolution brought to cities in Europe, we have viewed cities as a "necessary evil." Our dream has been a house in the bush or country — but close enough to the city so we can raid it for consumer goods and cultural experiences. We have built expressways into our city heart to make this plundering easier.

But we have been robbing ourselves blind.

We have pillaged and burned our own house.

Our home in the bush or country has been quickly swallowed up by the ever-spreading city as others also claim their piece of the "good life." We have been forced into longer and longer commutes in our car and into being full-time chauffeurs for our children. Increased traffic and added demand for parking lots have strangled many of our cities. What we have ended up with is neither a city nor the country — what many writers describe as "NoPlace." We have destroyed both the natural environment and the essential nature of the city.

Looking To the Future

Placing higher value on both the city and the country

In Western cultures, we have created a battleground between the city and the natural environment. We feel like we are forced to make a choice: city or country? Nostalgia, coupled with our anti-city sentiment, biases us towards choosing the country. But we have been forcing ourselves to make a false choice.

Tony Hiss, in *The Experience of Place*, discusses three different types of landscapes:

- *Natural or primeval landscapes*: not significantly altered by human intervention
- *Working landscapes*: shaped by human intervention over time but in cooperation with nature — farmland, fishing villages
- *Manufactured or urban landscapes*: cities and large urban areas.

Hiss explains how each of these landscapes has a special way of connecting with the human psyche:

- Natural or primeval landscapes create a sense of kinship with all of life
- Working landscapes create a sense of partnership with nature

Indeed, the car was often the best means for getting away from home and resettling elsewhere — as it was for the Okies who left their dust-blown farms in "rolling junks" and set out for California. To them, the car was more than a symbol of freedom; it embodied the elemental need of living creatures to flee adversity and seek a new home where they might thrive .... And since the car was the intrument of their deliverance to this promised land, it is little wonder that these newcomers to Los Angeles and their decendents enshrined it as an object of near religious worship in the years ahead.

James Howard Kunstler, *The Geography of Nowhere*

America does not yet fully accept urban life .... One day we may realize, as did the ancient Athenians, that the good life means the good city.

Kenneth Schneider, On the Nature of Cities

- Urban landscapes create a sense of kinship with our fellow humans.

To maximize personal growth, we need a relationship with all three types of landscape. While we may choose one of these landscapes as our prefered place of abode, we need access to the other two landscapes to maintain an inner balance. For this to happen, the integrity and accessibility of all three landscapes must be preserved. This means that cities cannot be allowed to spread out, destroying valuable farmland and natural landscapes. Cities that spread themselves thinly over the landscape destroy all three landscapes. They deny the essential nature of the city and are therefore not truly "cities." They are "anti-cities" — a cancer that destroys cities, working landscapes, and the natural environment.

Reclaiming our streets must therefore be part of a larger vision to reclaim our cities, our working landscapes, and the natural environment.

The need for adventure and roots

The city epitomizes an interesting paradoxical pull within the human psyche. We love adventure and exploring. But we also need roots: the warmth and security of "home."

This pull has been with us from early in our evolution. As hunters we roamed with the animals. We needed aggression to survive. As gardeners we learnt the value of cooperating with nature, the value of nurture and home. These paradoxical pulls are built into our streets. When using streets for movement, we are giving vent to our need for exploring and adventure. When using the streets for conversation, play, celebrations, people-watching, and commerce, we are giving vent to our need for a sense of home. If we have elevated the movement function of our streets to the point where it is jeopardizing the other functions, then we are denying one of our most fundamental needs: our need for a sense of home.

Reclaiming our streets must be therefore done in such a way that we strike a better balance between our need for exploring and adventure and our need for a sense of home. Street reclaiming does not entail denying our need for adventure and exploration. In fact, one of its goals is to turn every journey into a journey of adventure and discovery. But that can only happen if our streets are lively, ever-changing, and spontaneous.

Beyond Nostalgia

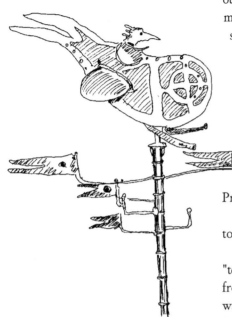

Dare to imagine —
And then dare to create.

I started this book by exploring a lost tradition, a tradition lost in the mechanization of our cities. But we must beware of nostalgia that simply pines for a lost age. There was much that was wrong with the streets of the past. The great challenge is to take the streets that we have *now* — streets that have been designed primarily as machines to move vehicles — and to reclaim them as places that facilitate personal and community growth. We can find clues for how we may do this by looking to the past. We may even find inspiration. But what we are currently presented with is a unique challenge that has no precedent in history.

In a sense we need to combine *re*-claiming with *pro*-claiming. Reclaiming takes back something lost. Proclaiming goes beyond just restoring something lost. It creates a new reality which is bigger, more innovative, more life-enhancing, more succulent, and more stimulating than anything that has gone before. Proclaiming is also about shouting a message — pointing the way to a new future.

How we create the streets of the future is up to us. This book has not pretended to have all the answers. It is a primer — a stimulus — for creating our own future.

The next few years will see an explosion in traffic reduction and street reclaiming "technologies." These will emerge from neighbourhoods like yours. They will emerge from people like you sitting down over a bottle of wine or a coffee and discussing ways to reclaim their street. They will emerge from dreams in the night and flights of fantasy.

They will not emerge if we see reducing traffic as some chore to be endured. They will only emerge if we begin celebrating a vision of what our streets could be like. They will not emerge if we mount our high horses and aim our lances at trucks and cars. They will emerge from the chatter and laughter of children playing in the street.

I invite you on a great adventure — the reclaiming of your street. This adventure starts in the playground of your own mind. Here you are god. Here you can build any kind of future you desire.

History is the story of those who dared to dream.

The future belongs to those who dare to create.

APPENDICES

HOW YOUR CLASS CAN WIN A

Traffic BUSTER PARTY

✔ Less Traffic
✔ Slower Speed
✔ Becter Neighbourhoods

2 Traffic Buster Parties to be Won

◆ Best Score Card on a Survey Day
◆ Most improved Score Card

By being a TRAFFIC BUSTER
you earn stars for your Class Score Card

Traffic Busters also get this cool sticker!

I'M A ★★ Traffic BUSTER

 ONE STAR TRAFFIC BUSTER
4 or more students sharing one car
Find other students that live near you and organise car-sharing buddies.

 TWO STAR TRAFFIC BUSTER
Walk -- Cycle -- Public Transport
Why not organise a Walking Bus?
Organise a Cycle Train.
Find a Public Transport Buddy to travel with.

BEWARE!! THE SURVEY DAYS CAN HAPPEN ANY DAY!!

Appendix 1: Reducing School Traffic

In 1997 I ran a trial of the *Traffic Reduction Kit* with two schools in a precinct of three private schools in Brisbane. While the process was different from that used in the *Traffic Reduction Kit*, the principles were the same. The major concern of the schools was safety for children, particularly because the schools shared some facilities and children had to cross back and forth across a road — used as a major rat-run — to access these shared facilities.

The process started with getting a base measure of how children were arriving at the school. Each class completed a simple survey which asked them how they had come to school that day and, if they had arrived by car, how many students had been in the car.

There was then an educational phase where each class watched an information video and generated ideas for solutions. I offered a pizza party to the class that came up with the best display of ideas.

Parents were invited to an *Ideas Party* where they watched a video and generated some initial ideas for solutions to the problem. Both the students and parents were told very clearly that the solutions had to include

- a reduction in the number of vehicles delivering children to the school
- management of the traffic that did remain.

A newsletter was also sent to local residents inviting them to the *Ideas Party* as some of the management solutions could have impacts on them. From this process a consensus did emerge on a plan for managing the traffic that remained. The street between the three schools was to be declared a *Virtual Car Free Zone*. Parents would agree to drop their kids at set-down and pick-up zones outside of this area. The idea was eventually to reclaim the space in the *Virtual Car Free Zone* with landscaping and facilities for the schools. This plan was presented to all parents in a newsletter and ratified. Street-corner meetings were held with local residents to explain the plan.

To reduce the number of vehicles arriving at the school, I worked directly with the children by running a *Traffic Buster Pizza Party Competition*. Over a four week period, I held random surveys of how the children had arrived at school (the same survey that was used to establish the base measure). Children who had walked or cycled earned two *Traffic Buster Stars* and got an appropriate sticker. Children who arrived in a car with four or more students received one *Traffic Buster Star* and an appropriate sticker. The stars for each class were totalled and converted into a score — number of stars per ten students. Using the base data collected earlier, I offered a pizza party as a prize to the class that improved the most and the class that got the highest score. People caught lying would disqualify their class from the competition.

The *Traffic Buster Competition* resulted in an overall drop of 11% in traffic generated by the two schools. There was a 33% increase in the number of children walking and a 21% increase in public transport usage. These results were significant given that before the trials began, parents said that there could be no reduction in the number of cars because these were private schools that drew students from all over Brisbane. An analysis of the surveys indicated that in the initial four weeks, only half of the potential reductions were actually achieved.

The reaction of the teachers was interesting. When I first spoke to them about their part in the educational process, there was not a great deal of enthusiasm. They already had high work loads. However, the teachers became increasingly enthusiastic and some worked very closely with students to go well beyond what was originally asked of them. For example, one teacher worked with her students to develop the idea of getting the parents to drop the students even further from the school than the designated drop-off zones. This was aimed at helping reduce congestion around the school even further. One teacher began riding his bike once a week and another started the first Walking Bus.

As in the neighbourhood trial, the school community became very keen to be involved in both the physical implementation and the maintenance and even in paying for their street reclaiming.

Unfortunately, Brisbane City Council did not continue the funding of this school trial and balked at the idea of the schools doing their own street reclaiming. Instead they decided to do their own calming works around the schools. However, the experiment did prove that the general principle I have outlined in this book can be applied successfully to schools. The important doorway into this process is the concern that parents have for the safety of their children in the school precinct — a concern that is heightened by the fact that so many parents drive their children to school.

In every city I hear the same story: in school holidays, traffic levels drop significantly. You will remember that I argued that the ease with which you can get traffic reductions is layered, the first 20% being extremely easy. I believe that school-based traffic is part of this first 20% and should be one of the primary targets of city-based reduction programs.

Appendix 2: An Economic Prosperity Plan

I believe that business could be used as a major driver of traffic reduction in cities. Cities could work with business in developing an **opportunities framework** which could be used as a way of promoting investment in traffic reduction. This framework may include the following components:

- *New Business Sectors — Direct investment opportunities*: In the last 15 years, leveraging savings through resource management has become a multi-billion dollar industry in trash recycling, energy conservation, and water conservation. Traffic reduction, as a sector of this resource management industry, is largely still in the conception stages (apart from Car Sharing Clubs which are a large business in Europe). Yet traffic reduction has the potential to far outstrip trash recycling in its dollar value. Traffic reduction technologies include the Walking Bus, Traffic Reduction Savings Brokers, SmartMove Rewards Card, leveraging of savings to Government authorities, and a host of yet-to-be-invented technologies such as the hybrid public transport system I envisaged earlier.

- *Indirect investment opportunities:* These center mainly on investment opportunities due to changed spending patterns. Traffic reduction promotes a stronger neighborhood-based economy (as opposed to a large regional facilities economy). This provides significant investment opportunities in new types of housing and retail, including "car-free urban villages." In addition, reduced car use requires fewer car parking spaces on private property. This valuable resource can be "re-used" for activities with a higher earning potential (more shops, housing, office space, etc.)

- *Direct cost-savings to businesses:* Businesses can save significant money through reducing their own vehicle use; better utilizing their employees' time; reducing freight movement costs due to reduced congestion; and better rationalizing freight movement.

- *Indirect cost-savings:* A more efficient urban form reduces infrastructure costs to all levels of government which reduces levels of taxation to business.

- *Indirect increases to cash income:* Traffic reduction increases the level of disposable income within the local and regional economy. (Money spent burning fuel tends to migrate out of the local economy.) Traffic reduction will also improve the amenity of a city. Amenity is fast becoming the number one determinant of where businesses locate or relocate. These new businesses increase the potential cash flow for existing businesses.

- *Direct schemes to increase cash income:* Businesses may attract a larger share of the disposable income created by traffic reduction by promoting themselves as supporters of traffic reduction (much as environmental concern has led to new marketing strategies for a range of consumer products.) For example, a business may offer a discount to people who belong to *Traffic Reduction Treaty Streets* and shop locally. Neighborhood businesses may band together in such a scheme to promote the neighborhood shopping centre.

- *Green Tourism:* The cities to become leaders in traffic reduction will increase their international profile. A whole new area of green tourism could be generated: planning professionals, students, concerned citizens, and decision-makers who come to these cities to investigate traffic reduction. To boost this tourist trade, an *International Traffic Reduction Conference* may be held each year. Part of the plan may be to document carefully all aspects of the city's traffic reduction program to be put on permanent display in a *Traffic Reduction Study Center.*

The economic prosperity plan should also contain **Government Initiatives** including

- *Means of leveraging a proportion of wealth-creation* to reinvest in order to encourage higher levels of traffic reduction and associated business activity.

- *Mechanisms for reinvesting a proportion of savings* accruing to city councils from traffic reduction in order to leverage further reductions in traffic. Savings accrue in reduced — direct and indirect — infrastructure costs. (Sprawling cities require higher levels of investment in water, sewerage, roads, public transport, electricity, etc.) A proportion of these savings can be reinvested in order to buy further reductions in traffic which produce even greater levels of saving.

- *City Council Policies and Initiatives* which will support and encourage business investment in traffic reduction. These initiatives may include partnerships with the business community.

SELECT BIBLIOGRAPHY

Alexander, Christopher et al., *A Pattern Language: Towns, Buildings, Construction.* New York: Oxford University Press, 1977.

Anon., *Holy Bible: New International Version.* East Brunswick: New International Bible Society, 1973.

Appleyard, Donald, *Livable Streets.* Berkeley: University of California Press, 1981.

Bacon, Edmund N. *Design of Cities.* New York: Penguin Books, 1976.

Banks, Robert. *The Tyranny of Time.* Sydney: Lancer, 1985.

Brambilla, Roberto, *More Streets for People.* The Italian Art and Landscape Foundation, 1975.

Breheny, M. and A. Hooper (Eds.) *Rationality in Planning: Critical Essays on the Role of Rationality in Urban and Regional Planning.* London: Pion, 1985.

Cartwright, T.J. "Planning and Chaos Theory," *Journal of the American Planning Association* 57, No 1, (winter 1991) pp.44–56.

Crowhurst-Lennard, Suzanne and Henry L. Lennard, "Public Life in Urban Places: the Lessons of the Venetian Campo," *Stepping Out in Urban Design: The Sixth Annual Pedestrian Conference Proceedings.* Boulder: Transportation Division, City of Boulder, 1985.

Cunningham, Chris, *Towards a New Planning Framework: A Philosophical Response to David Engwicht's Proposal.* Unpublished paper, 1994.

Cunningham, Chris and Martin Auster, *Urban Design and Regulation.* Armidale: Department of Geography and Planning, University of New England, 1992.

Davis, Mike, *City of Quartz: Excavating the Future in Los Angeles.* London: Vintage, 1990.

Engwicht, David, *Towards an Eco-City: Calming the Traffic.* Sydney: Envirobook, 1992 (Published 1993 as *Reclaiming Our Cities & Towns: Better Living with Less Traffic.* Philadelphia: New Society Publishers).

—— *Traffic Calming: The Solution to Route 20 and a New Vision for Brisbane.* Brisbane: CART, 1989.

Fishman, Robert, *Urban Utopias in the Twentieth Century: Ebenezer Howard, Frank Lloyd Wright, and Le Corbusier.* Cambridge: The MIT Press, 1982.

Gardner, Howard, *Creating Minds: An Anatomy of Creativity Seen Through the Lives of Freud, Einstein, Picasso, Stravinsky, Eliot, Graham, and Gandhi.* Basic Books, 1993.

Garreau, Joel, *Edge City: Life on the New Frontier.* New York: Anchor Books, 1992.

Gleick, James, *Chaos: Making a New Science.* London: Sphere Books, 1990.

Goleman, Daniel, *Vital Lies, Simple Truths: The Psychology of Self-Deception.* London: Bloomsbury, 1998.

—— *Emotional Intelligence: Why It Can Matter More than IQ.* London: Bloomsbury, 1996.

Gratz, Roberta Brandes, *The Living City.* New York: Simon and Schuster, 1989.

Greed, Clara H., *Women and Planning: Creating Gendered Realities.* London: Routledge, 1994.

Greenberg, Mike, *The Poetics of Cities: Designing Neighborhoods that Work.* Columbus: Ohio State University Press, 1995.

Hall, Peter, *Cities of Tomorrow: An Intellectual History of Urban Planning and Design in the Twentieth Century.* Oxford: Basil Blackwell, 1988.

Hart, Stanley I. and Alvin L. Spivak, *Automobile Dependence and Denial: The Elephant in the Bedroom: Impacts on the Economy and Environment.* Pasadena: New Paradigm Books, 1993.

Haymann, Nathalie, *Resumed in Protest: The Human Cost of Roads.* Sydney: Bungoona Books, 1994.

Hillier, Bill and Julienne Hanson, *The Social Logic of Space.* Cambridge: Cambridge University Press, 1990.

Hiss, Tony, *The Experience of Place: A New Way of Looking at and Dealing With Our Radically Changing Cities and Countryside.* New York: Vintage Books, 1991.

Illich, Ivan, *Energy and Equity.* London: Marion Boyars, 1976.

Jacobs, Jane, *The Death and Life of Great American Cities.* New York: Random House, 1961.

Jackson, John Brinckerhoff, *Discovering the Vernacular Landscape.* New Haven: Yale University Press, 1984.

King, Graham A.D., "No Particular Place: A Meditation on Mobility", *The Planner TCPSS Proceedings,* (23 February, 1990) pp.43–46.

Koestler, Arthur, *The Act of Creation.* London: Pan Books, 1970.

Kunstler, James Howard, "Fighting Words from the US of A," *Urban Design Forum,* No. 43, (September 1999) p.1, 1998.

—— *The Geography of Nowhere: The Rise and Decline of America's Man-Made Landscape.* New York: Simon and Schuster, 1993.

Landry, Charles and Franco Bianchini, *The Creative City.* London: Demos, 1995.

McNulty, Robert et al., *Return of the Livable City in America.* Partners for Livable Places, Washington, DC: Acropolis Books, 1986.

Manning, Ian, *Beyond Walking Distance: The Gains from Speed in Australian Urban Travel.* Canberra: Urban Research Unit, Australian National University, 1984.

Marsh, Peter and Peter Collet, "Driving Passion," *Psychology Today* (June 1987) pp.16–24.

Meller, Helen, *Patrick Geddes: Social Evolutionist and City Planner.* London: Routledge, 1993.

Mumford, Lewis, *The Myth of the Machine: Technics and Human Development.* New York: Harcourt, Brace and Word, 1967.

—— *The City in History: Its Origins, Its Transformations, and Its Prospects.* London: Penguin Books, 1961.

Nachmanovitch, Stephen, *Free Play: Improvisation in Life and Art.* New York: Tarcher & Putnam Books, 1990.

Newman, Peter and Jeff Kenworthy, *Cities and Automobile Dependence: An International Source Book.* Albershot: Gower Technical, 1989.

Nuttgens, Patrick, Floris Van Den Broecke, Jane Heath, and John Houston, *The Furnished Landscape: Applied Art in Public Places.* London: Bellew Publishing, 1992.

Oakeshott, Michael, *Rationalism in Politics and Other Essays.* New York: Methuen & Co, Barnes and Noble Books, 1962.

TEST, *Quality Streets: How Traditional Urban Centers Benefit from Traffic Calming.* London: TEST, 1988.

Tranter, Paul, *Children's Mobility in Canberra: Confinement or Independence?* Canberra: University College, The University of New South Wales, Australian Defence Force Academy, 1993.

Roberts, Ian et al., *Pedalling Health: Health Benefits of a Modal Transport Shift.* Adelaide: Department of Transport, South Australian State Bicycle Committee, 1995.

Roberts, John, "Genius Loci: How Is It Retained or Revived?" *Getting There, By All Means: Eighth Annual Pedestrian Conference.* Boulder: City of Boulder Transportation Division, 1987.

Rudofsky, Bernard, *Architecture Without Architects: A Short Introduction to Non-Pedigreed Architecture.* Albuquerque: University of New Mexico Press, 1990.

——*Streets for People: A Primer for Americans.* New York: Doubleday, 1969.

Rueda, Salvador et al., *The Sustainable City.* Barcelona: Centre de Cultura Contemporania de Barcelona, 1998.

St Clair, David J., *The Motoerization of American Cities*. New York: Praeger, 1986

Schneider, Kenneth R., *On the Nature of Cities*. San Francisco: Jossey-Bass Publications, 1979.

SEARCH Residents Group, *Brisbane Traffic Management: An Alternative Approach*. Brisbane: SEARCH Residents Group Inc., 1991.

Sennett, Richard, *The Conscience of the Eye: The Design and Social Life of Cities*. New York: Alfred A. Knopf, 1990.

—— Lane, Alen, *The Uses of Disorder: Personal Identity and City Life*. London: The Penguin Press, 1971.

—— (Ed.) *Classic Essays on the Culture of Cities*. London: Prentice-Hall, 1969.

Specter, David Kenneth, *Urban Spaces*. New York: New York Graphic Society, 1974.

Tambiah, Stanley Jeyaraja, *Magic, Science, Religion, and the Scope of Rationality*. Cambridge: Cambridge University Press, 1990.

Tanghe, Jan, Sieg Vlaeminck and Jo Berghoef, *Living Cities: A Case for Urbanism and Guidelines for Re-urbanization*. Oxford: Pergamon Press, 1984.

Tolley, Rodney (Ed.), *The Greening of Urban Transport: Planning for Walking and Cycling in Western Cities*. London: Belhaven Press, 1990.

Tranter, Paul J., *Children's Mobility in Canberra: Confinement or Independence*. Canberra: Department of Geography and Oceanography, University of New South Wales, 1993

Tranter, Paul J. and John W. Doyle, "Reclaiming the Residential Street as Play Space," *International Play Journal*, 4, (1996) pp.81–97.

Van der Ryn, Sim and Peter Calthorpe, *Sustainable Communities: A New Design Synthesis for Cities, Suburbs, and Towns*. San Francisco: Sierra Club Books, 1991.

Wackernagel, Mathis and William Rees, *Our Ecological Footprint: Reducing Human Impact on the Earth*. Gabriola Island, BC: New Society Publishers, 1996.

Whitelegg, John, "Time Pollution," *The Ecologist*, Vol 23, No 4, (1993) pp.131–134.

Whyte, William H., *City: Rediscovering the Center*. New York: Anchor Books, 1990.

Wildavsky, Aaron, "If Planning is Everything, Maybe it's Nothing", *Policy Sciences*, 4 (1973) pp.127–153.

Wilson, Elizabeth, *The Sphinx in the City: Urban Life, the Control of Disorder, and Women*. London: Virago Press, 1991.

INDEX